Stuck U.

The 5-Step Course to Unlocking Your Inner Awesome

DR. BRIDGET COOPER

Cover art by Dr. Bridget Cooper. Cover design by Kelly Gineo.

ISBN-13: 978-0692395653
ISBN-10: 0692395652

DEDICATION

This book is dedicated to the young women who challenge me daily
to stay emotionally agile and forever hopeful:
my daughters, Jessica and Elena.
May you always know your true strength, and
experience the abundant blessings of your inner awesome.

3-22-16

Erina,

May your challenges be outnumbered by your resources! ♡

Peace,

Beth

CONTENTS

TRIBUTES

"I attribute my success to this:
I never gave or took any excuse." ~ Florence Nightingale

Who doesn't love Florence Nightingale? Writing a book like this forces you to challenge yourself about where you do and don't model the lessons you're teaching. It also invites you to challenge others in the same way, whether they appreciate it or not! There are so many people who are a part of this book, from its inception to its publication. My hope is that this pays tribute to them fully and fairly.

Most importantly, to my phenomenal, beautiful, and precocious daughters, Jessica & Elena: You teach me every day about the process of change. I am blessed to witness your growth into powerful young women, and I am transformed as I try to guide you by example. I am passionate about every last speck of each of you and pray that you welcome change as part of life's journey. The path *is* the destination, my loves.

To Lisa: We have walked together through so many changes in our lives and I couldn't dream of a better ally, advocate, and confidante. Your clarity and candid nature challenge me to be a better person, day in and day out. Thank you for reminding me to laugh…and cry. I can't wait till I hand you my glass of water as I walk out on stage…

To Joe: Talk about paths…I owe you so much for serving as an example of the challenges that change presents, even when we hold so much passion for it. Thank you for encouraging me and being my staunch cheerleader and task master when I get off-track or chase bright, shiny objects. You were my strength when I was weak and I am forever grateful. Yes, you are the wind beneath my tattered wings.

To the colleagues and clients I've had the pleasure to advise and serve over the years: Your stories are woven throughout this book.

You taught me so much about human nature and the power of the system when it comes to change. Thank you for trusting me to assist you in transforming your businesses, and your approach to life. You've allowed me to influence your change process and your lives. I am honored and humbled. This model is grounded in our work together!

To my advance reviewers (especially my Auntie Joanie!): Thank you for taking the time and energy to read my manuscript, even under a ridiculously short deadline. I deeply appreciate your feedback and commentary and I hope that this book helped you to open up your #pipelineofawesome!

To Kelly, my cover designer: Thank you for being my creative guru and for having the patience of Job as I recreated it over and over under such tight time constraints! I know I can be a complete pain in the arse and I so appreciate you being so talented *and* understanding.

To my professors at UConn: You asked me many years ago, "How does change occur?" I knew way back then that I only had part of the answer so I searched for the keys that led me to this book. Thank you for being the seed that grew into this tree that will serve so many. Isn't that what we envisioned after all?

To the negative forces throughout my life: I thank you for showing me the value of change and the dangers inherent in being stuck. Your pain, and the pain you brought to me, strengthens me and my resolve to help change the world, one person at a time. I am grateful every day for your presence in my journey and I hope that your path becomes one of freedom and growth.

To you, the reader: I hope you see enough of yourself in the pages that you make this your manual for transforming anything and everything that displeases you in your work and life. Thank you for inspiring me to share this guide for managing and directing your change process. You only have one shot at this thing called life: Take it. Now, go unlock your inner awesome!

"Each morning we are born again.
What we do today is what matters most." ~ Buddha

FOREWORD

It all happened in about 2 seconds. That rush of thoughts. . .

. . . Working 35 hours a week . . . going to college full time (the first in my family's history) . . . commuting back and forth, as I did not have the funds to pay for housing. . . my father now in his 8th year suffering through multiple sclerosis while being nearly blind and unable to walk. . . the trapped feeling knowing you rely on Social Security disability income to keep a family of 5 going . . . wondering if switching majors is the right move. . . the cold and isolation driving the back roads after 10 PM that night. . . other stuff. . .

Since I am now writing this some 35 years later, I did avoid that tree, deciding to veer left and as hard as it seemed it to be that night, I kept to the road. I questioned that decision of "why" veer left for many miles too. Aimlessly at times I continued to wander through time, a potential career, pushing for grades, working late, etc. with nary a clue on how to move forward. Caught up in the false hope that doing what others did, or aspired to do, as a measure of potential success seemed like such a good idea.

The book you are about to read is from a person I had the honor to meet nearly 12 years ago as I started out on my own venture with a business advisory practice. Many of the words that you will read in this book will hit you square between the eyes. Yes, everyone. I know Bridget Cooper and she is not a wall flower. When you read this you may question if all her experiences were real or borrowed from those she helped. Let me say that I have yet to meet anyone - and I know about a thousand people very, very well - who has had to weather a colossal sh** storm more than Bridget. I knew what rained down on her and yes, they were all too true. She has worked her way through most of them and as a human being, still reports challenges that continue to find her. She tells you in these pages throughout her prose. She is not immune to what we all call "life." However, that "storm," her education, and her life's work delivers advice contained in these precious pages that will resonate with even the most "put together" folks. I suspect much of this advice will command your attention as you reflect on your path of life and you encounter obstacles, opportunities, choices, and decision "trees" going forward.

I learned, much the hard way as you may have figured by now, about things like "control buckets" which Bridget vividly paints so you know where you stand when it comes to influencing the world around you. I finally solved that one. Are you aware of a concept called (no pun intended) "Awareness?" I am. It took me 30 years to figure that one out. Ever have your fears take hold of you? Who hasn't? Can't tell you how many of those things I tripped over or ran over me that I eventually overcame. Solved most of those, too. . .

Alone.

I wish I knew then what I know *right now.* On one's journey through life, the best laid plans will be filled with pot holes and repaved with intentions and advice from others. Did you ever consider the fact that you might want to have a say in this? Ever know that there is a way to figure that out? "Stuck U." is that solution. Bridget outlines and fluently shares one of her concepts called "Emotional Agility." This is the key that will unlock the prison of the place you are in and will enable you to build a roadmap to find your way out – to the place YOU want to be. Is this the end-all solution? Nope. You have to put in most of the work. You knew that. And this is no surprise to anyone who reads any self-help or advice laden book. This one, however, is different.

Yeah, I know you've heard that phrase before. Many people who know me and my work understand and have witnessed how I can help find the uniqueness in any individual's business or on their personal resume. I know "different" and I help people find it every day. In Bridget's book, the "unique" difference is in the simplicity, elegance, and clarity with which she lays out the plan to examine *you* and allow you to move to a new place in *your* life. It is a method for you to find your way through life's maze. The method prescribes medicine that is not going to be tasty nor is it going to help right away. It is different because she will yell at you and often put you into a place where you just want to punch back. It is not going to be easy. It makes you move. It makes you change. You get to where you want to be.

So why would you listen to *anyone* who just tells you what you want to hear? My career has been fruitful and successful with most people, but an arrow in my quiver was always missing. I could not cross the line to help those who I could not help. I needed their business as a background, a balance sheet or, I had to defer the topic because I was entering territory where I was not licensed or educated to give advice even if the solution was readily apparent. Analogies and metaphors would not work. I saw people lost in their own world . . . seeing where they were . . . but not able to supply the navigational tools to help them escape.

With this book in hand, that arrow is now firmly in my grasp. If you are someone who is successful, make sure you have this arrow when you next face a "challenge." If you are that good, share it with those who do not have such a resource. If you are somewhere where you do not want to be, grab this book and delve into it to find that place where you got lost and begin your personal change. The start is that simple - *start.* The steps outlined in this book are fairly simple – follow them. They work because I have done it (the hard way!) and I have seen it. The effort you need to put in between each step can be consuming. Change is not easy. But I believe you already knew this.

Stuck U. is elegantly written and easy to comprehend. The analogies contained within are communicated from all facets of work and life. The quotes bring depth and breadth to concepts, action items and her experiential prose. After reading this book, and based on my experience with change, I am sure you will find yourself on one of these pages and wonder why you are doing things the way you are currently doing them. You might actually think of changing . . . perhaps once again. And this would be a good thing.

And after you read this book, you will discover why the world will be a better place.

Thomas R. Fleury
Executive Management & Business Care, LLC

South Windsor, CT
February 2015

"Try not to become a man of success,
but rather try to become a man of value." ~ Albert Einstein

1

PROLOGUE

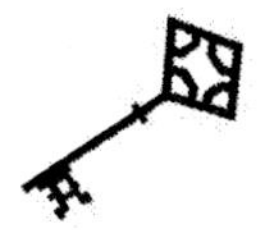

"The only place where success comes before work
is in the dictionary." ~ Vidal Sassoon

I am not a writer. Well, I suppose that makes little sense to you since here you are reading my book. Yet, it's true, at least in the conventional sense of the word. What am I, then? I am a communicator. A spokesperson. A passionate change agent. A thought leader, according to a recent post. Writing books is simply the vehicle for me to transmit my message, hopefully to the widest possible audience. And so it is with this book. My role is to be your Chief Asskicker: If you don't want it kicked, don't hand it to me. I take my role *very* seriously.

"It is in our darkest moments
that we must focus to see the light." ~Aristotle

Shortly after my first book was published in 2013, people started asking me when my next book was to be published. Next book? I was still feeling high from getting the first book out the door. Yet, anyone who knows me knows that I'd already thought about that and had convinced myself that putting a book out every two years was a solid plan. I'm not as prolific as Steven King once was, so I'm not sure why I set down this particular gauntlet? Once I've committed to something it's like pulling candy away from kids to get me to give up on it. Not happening. To make things a little easier, my mind never stops working. Ever. I mean it. I have somehow managed to calm my inner thoughts more of the time than not, but my internal dialogue is quite comical in its speed and the trails it blazes. Writing it all down is simply an exercise in focus, dedication, and organization.

But why this book? Why did I want to write about change and Emotional Agility? Why did I think that *this* was the book that needed to be written? The thought occurred to me one day as I was scanning all of the motivational posts on everyone's Facebook™ newsfeeds, and pondering how many of those people weren't living the essence of what that quote intended. They were posting things like, "Don't allow people to take advantage of you, you're better than that," yet, I knew them personally and their middle name might as well have been "doormat" or "kick me, please."

But the quotes! They work! If you say them (and better yet, post them), they are true! If you know you shouldn't be treated like trash, you won't be! Right? Apparently not. Day after day, year after year, we witness people in our lives (and ourselves) reenacting the same unhealthy patterns, despite all of this "awareness" of what the right answer is. We witness others (and ourselves!) being stuck, despite their protests that they know better.

Having studied human behavior intensely for as long as I can remember, I knew I had answers to this predicament. I know that my answers can enlighten people and motivate them to make powerful shifts that could transform their lives. Rapidly. Comprehensively. And permanently. I provided a heap of insight and a call to action in *Feed The Need* (2013, 2014), yet I wasn't sure if I'd properly tackled how to bring those insights into action. And insight without action is like an award-winning recipe with no kitchen.

Welcome to the kitchen.

~ What If? ~

"The cave you fear to enter
holds the treasure you seek." ~ Joseph Campbell

Afraid yet? If you're like most people, the word "change" elicits fear, or at least a healthy dose of anxiety. When things are the same and predictable, we feel safer. We know what is expected of us and we can act accordingly. If you've always been the one to bring the pumpkin pie to Thanksgiving dinner and suddenly you're on turkey duty, you're filled with trepidation. What if you mess it up? What if it's dry? Or you don't buy a big enough bird? Or? Or? Or? To considering changing anything, including our contribution to a holiday meal, we require some measure of confidence and calm; knowing that things will work out okay. If you have strong Emotional Agility, you will welcome change more readily. You will be a master of change; not fearless, but courageous. Sound inviting?

The world is changing at a phenomenal and unprecedented rate. Most of us feel like we can't keep up. It's requiring us to think in different ways and do new things to approach novel problems. Our world is screaming out for us to be emotionally agile: to manage new experiences, changing circumstances, fresh information, and the stress that emerges in calm and tactical ways. *Stuck U* is the roadmap and the support system necessary to bring you to the major leagues of Emotional Agility.

If you're a company executive, this is the change manual you must distribute to your employees. How do you unstick a team? If your staff isn't onboard, your change efforts just went out the window, along with your wallet. This book guides them to get onboard and be a catalyst for change and not the status quo. Your company isn't made up of drones and robots. Your company is comprised of people. Work is personal. There are complex relationships in your office place.

People spend more time with their colleagues than they do their families in many cases.

Your organizational change isn't going to happen without *each individual* changing. You have to invest in THEIR change process in order for them to invest in YOUR change process. Have you ever had a trouble employee and you offered them every opportunity to fix themselves and they didn't? There's no doubt that you found that incredibly frustrating. What was missing? Choice. It was their *choice* not to change. Influence their choice in a proactive, authentic manner and you'll be way ahead of the competition.

As I spoke about in *Feed The Need*, people bring their craziness to work with them. We all carry our crazy around with us everywhere we go. You can deny or marginalize the role that emotions and crazy behavior play in your organizational success, or, you can own that bitch. Use the principles and lessons in this book and buckle up for your company's meteoric rise.

In this book, you're going to learn how to take your insights and put them into action. You'll be poised to use all those quotes you've been recounting and sharing for years and actually live their truth. It's not necessarily going to be easy. For some, it'll come hard and suddenly. For others, it'll be a slow and steady tortoise race. Either way, this book will provide you with the basis and the support to guide you through to the existence that has eluded you to this point, and not for your lack of effort. We just hadn't met yet.

Please don't waste another precious second of your temporary existence on hesitation. I hate to be the bearer of truth, but you're not getting any younger. And, your problems aren't likely to fix themselves. If you're problem-free and you're just looking to improve for the sake of more success and happiness, well, that's not going to just happen unless you have a fairy godmother I'm unaware of. (If you do, please send her my way. I can keep her very, very busy. Thank you!).

I'm ready to rock and roll. Are you?

2

THE BASICS

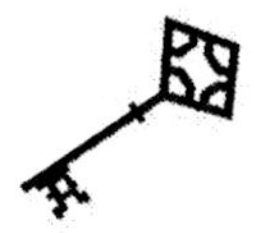

"Change is the law of life. And those who look only to the past are certain to miss the future."
~ President John F. Kennedy

Change sucks. It's painful and scary and it's everywhere. If you're like so many of us, you have all the advice and cute quotes and lists everywhere: on Facebook™, LinkedIn™, your office wall, etc. Then why are we still so unhappy? And stuck? And continuing to repeat the same pains over and over? Everywhere you look you see inspirational quotes, self-help mantras, and books on how to improve everything from your career progression to your sex life to your relationship with your mother. Companies invest millions of dollars undertaking change management initiatives and many experience lackluster results. So why are people generally unhappy, unfulfilled, and complaining about their lot in life? And, why do these things we seek to improve seemingly always circle the same drain? If we have all the answers, why do we keep seeking new solutions? Why does everything seem to stay the same? What is the missing link?

It's simple. It's change, or the lack thereof. We are all talking a good game about being in different circumstances, happier, and all sorts of "less" this and "more" that. Less angry, resentful, frustrated, impatient, fat, moody, broke, unsuccessful, and so on. More forgiving, energetic, upbeat, peaceful, self-confident, in shape, and on and on. We seem to want these changes. We talk about it, post about it, complain about it, beat ourselves up about it. But the "it" stays out of our grasp. What if you could grab ahold of "it" and make "it" happen, for real? For good? What if you could leave that limbo state experience in the past and be empowered to shift and change in any way you see fit?

I'm going to pose the question that has plagued people smarter than me for a good, long time. Do people really change? That's a big question. Companies spend big money on change management. But who gets the individuals who comprise the company to change? To get invested? In more cases than not, they aren't invested. There are abundant statistics out there to prove the point that, in general, people aren't connected to the purpose of the company or the work. It's no small wonder that so many businesses realize lackluster and roller coaster results; small hills really. What these companies need is a guide to get people signed on for the change…a map…and guidebook…a personal resource and talisman. And, drum roll, please. *Stuck U.* is here to provide all of that to anyone smart and fortunate enough to read and follow it.

In this book, you will gain the insight and the tools you need to craft your own destiny. You are in charge of you and what you make of yourself. Not your parents, not your boss, not your lover (or former lover or trail of former lovers or spouses), not the media, not some person or people who have harmed you along the way. You. Just you. Only you. YOU.

The only question that really matters at this point is, are you ready? Not sure? That's okay. The first chapter is devoted to getting you ready and sweeping out the cobwebs in your head that are clouding your vision of where you want to be. It's a scary proposition to be offered the keys to the castle you've been building in your head, fulfilling all the "if only" wishes you've held so dear. You don't believe me? You think that you'd love to be there in the castle, gazing out over the kingdom of happiness and wealth and emotional peace you keep talking about wanting? Well, I've got one simple question for you: Why the heck aren't you *there* already?

Do you think I might not understand what it means to be "stuck?" That I might not be compassionate to your story, what you've been through, and what you face? Think again. The details in each of our stories are different (a little or a lot) but the core of our stories have stunning similarities and common threads. It's reminds of that little factoid that when you look to your left and your right, both of those people share 99% of their DNA with you. We are more similar than different, regardless of the details we focus our attention on.

To illustrate my point, let me offer a narrative of what "stuck" can look like. See if you recognize yourself in it.

Example: I have a friend who is stuck in sloth mode. He is used to people being impatient with him. What has that done? It's made him passive aggressive in response. And it's calcified him into his "I come up short" inner dialogue (proving himself…and the voice he holds onto from his father…right). He doesn't know what to do when he's not being judged. Or pushed. It forces him to sit with himself and own up to his stall. He has to take responsibility for whatever he does, or doesn't do. He can't blame it on anyone. He has to own it. And he's not quick to move. Because moving forward has always been forced by the expectations of others. Without those expectations to thrust him into the next step, he's lost. And he's left wandering around in the dark trying to find out who he is and what he wants. Which is new for him, because those things were always defined for him in the past. Now he gets to craft his own identity and he's not sure who he is or what he wants or what he's capable of. And that is scary. Very scary.

When the world (or a certain person or group) is in control of you, there's an upside and a downside. The upside is that you don't have to take responsibility for much of anything and life is very predictable. The downside is the very same. My father spent most of his adult life in prison (mentally and literally) and I often wondered why a person would continue to do things that would land him in such a place? His drug addiction was certainly a major player. Plus, he loved to blame the police for "setting him up." Well, Dad, not sure I can let you off the hook since you *were* breaking the law in a number of ways regardless of how and when they caught you.

So, if it wasn't just his addiction and it wasn't the big, bad po-po (police), what was it? I believe it was safety. He knew what to expect in prison. He had three square meals a day, a place to sleep, and a system telling him what to do and when. He had never grown up and was lousy at being responsible for himself and all the details of a day-to-day existence. Prison removed all those obstacles. Prison took away most of his decision-making abilities. Making decisions is hard work, especially for some of us. Owning up to the outcome of our decisions is even tougher still.

Although my father was a criminal, his patterns aren't unlike those presented to many of us making our way in the world: We struggle with our demons and we blame the world for our troubles, yet somehow knowing deep down that we are creating our own sickness. Sound sad? It's quite the opposite, if we let it be. If we are responsible for creating our own sickness then we can be in charge of our own healing. We can transform ourselves into whatever we choose, just as we can limit ourselves to whatever degree we select. Do you think I'm lying (or delusional)? Nope. I'm being brutally honest. You're either the hero of your own story or the victim of it. Either way, it's your story. YOUR story. You're writing it, narrating it, and starring in it. Changing the ending (and every chapter leading up to it) is yours to create, to a great extent. Tragedy can befall us, just like great fortune and longevity can. But there is so much we can do along the way to define our outcomes. We can control and influence so much. Make today count for something. Something good.

Now, congratulations are in order, so, congratulations! You may feel and be stuck, but you got out of your own way long enough to buy this book and start *reading* it. I'm guessing you did all this because you want to make something (or maybe a whole host of things) different in your life. Maybe you've made some changes in the past but for some reason or another, you're stuck, energy depleted. You know something needs to change but you're not doing enough (or anything) about it.

You've got a billion excuses, I know. I'm sorry, *reasons*. Let's be honest with one another for just a minute, can we please? They are excuses that are holding you back, for the most part, anyway. I'm sure you've had struggles and walls built to keep you from your dreams. So how is it that other people have made it to where you envision yourself to be? Are they really that much more talented or lucky than you? My guess is probably not. Then what is their answer?

In most cases it's a basic difference that separates those who are living a happy, fulfilling life: they decided to. They made their minds up that the life they wanted was worth setting aside all the things that promised to hold them back from their "it." They stopped thinking so much about the "why nots" and focused on the "why." They moved forward instead of standing still. Each time they had an opportunity to remain complacent and complain about their recent failure or upset, they chose to pick themselves up and move on. They *decided* to.

~ Easy as Pie ~

"The only thing standing between you and your goal
is the bullshit story you keep telling yourself as to
why you can't achieve it." ~ Jordan Belfort

So, *that's* the secret? Decision making? Yup, sure is. It's deciding to change your mind about things that might be tough to let go of. It's deciding that the cost of staying where you are is greater than the cost of pursuing a different present and future. It's deciding to change your way of thinking about yourself, others, and the world so you can change your behavior. When you truly, really, and deeply decide to change, you can.

They say people don't change. I say that's bull. People do change, sometimes 180 degrees from where they started. It doesn't take monumental shifts to change the course of your entire life. It's done in baby steps. In slight degree shifts. In repetitive actions. In staying the course. In seeing that the benefits of being unstuck are greater than the benefits of sitting still.

You are the sum of all of your choices to this point: Your choices to move and your choices to be still. You are who and where you are as a result of your actions and your inactions. A choice is simply the action that follows a decision. Decision making is what keeps us up at night and running around in circles in the daylight. "What should I do?" is a question you probably ask yourself a dozen or more times a day, and that's just consciously.

Why do people fret over every decision facing them? It's simple. We fear making mistakes. Which, let me tell you, is *such* a waste of time and energy. Our mistakes make us who we are. Bad relationships teach us what we DON'T want in the next one. Horrible jobs make us thankful for a good one. I'm not recommending that we be foolish in our choices, but making ourselves crazy trying to avoid making a mistake IS a mistake. And not making a decision IS a decision.

I was driving my car the other day around town, returning home from completing some errands and it struck me. All of the people in all of the houses I was passing are going through all sorts of motions to get the work done necessitated by our societal norms. But, do they realize that it's all temporary? That their life could be over later today or tomorrow or in five or ten short years? That no matter how long their life is, it will "soon" be over? So, what does it matter if their lawn is the greenest on the block? Or if they have newly painted siding and a trendy new walkway? And all the people working for companies, pushing paper and having meetings and producing some widget…are they asking themselves "what does it matter?"

This thought bothered me deeply. Super deeply. It's the sort of question that give people insomnia, including me. What's the meaning of all of this "busy-ness" of our "business?" My hypothesis is that being "busy" and caught up in the monotony of the getting through the demands of our daily life keeps us safe from considering that we are all so very temporary on this planet. When we leave this Earth, we will also leave behind a to-do list and countless things that we were on our way to do that will now need to be done by someone else. And, that "someone else" will leave the very same way.

Now, please don't get me wrong. I'm not advocating that you *not* take good care of your lawn, house, job, children, and self. By all means, please do. What I *am* advocating is that you pause to consider what truly brings you joy, gives your life meaning, and makes you feel wholly alive and passionate. Figure out a way to do more of that than anything else. Make THAT the center of your life. Not the lawn. Unless lawn maintenance makes you feel alive and passionate and gives your life meaning. Then have at it! And, please honestly consider expanding your reach and spending some time at my house because my lawn could really use your love.

In any event, read this loud and clear: You are temporary. Your time on this planet is fleeting. This is powerful news because it means that all the busy things you do are far less important than you've been building them up to be. All the dramas and arguments and wrinkles and bruises and bumps are really just inconveniences and distractions from what is really worth your time and energy and love.

They don't really matter in the end. If they don't matter in the end, why on Earth do they matter now? Pause on that for a minute. It's a profoundly new way of thinking about things for most people. They don't matter. So, what can you do? Try this exercise.

Exercise: Close your eyes (yes, after you finishing reading this passage, wise guy) and imagine how amazing and successful and joyous those things you are passionate about could be today if you used your energy and your love to build them instead of feeding your dramas and insecurities. Jot down an estimate of how much time just over the past week that you've spent:

- Doing mundane tasks that really don't build anything of meaning in your life?
- Arguing with or playing out angry or victim-oriented thoughts about other people?
- Circling the emotional or mental drain, beating yourself up about something or other?
- Procrastinating doing what you dream about accomplishing? Starting sentences with "someday…?"

Remember: Choice got you into the mess you're in, and choice can lead you back out. Maintain a solution-focus: What is standing in the way of me getting the outcome I want? What can I do to remove those barriers? If you focus on the problem, you'll be blind to your choices. If you focus on the possible solutions, you'll empower yourself to take charge and influence the outcome.

"The sign of intelligence is that you are constantly wondering.
Idiots are always dead sure about every damn thing
they are doing in their life." ~ Vasudev

~ Stop This Carousel, I Want To Get Off! ~

"I must be willing to give up what I am
in order to become what I will be." ~ Albert Einstein

You are stuck. You're in a rut. You're having a tough time in one or more areas of your life and you need to fix that. You're on a merry-go-round of dysfunction or unrest or simply not rising to your inborn potential. Your company is requiring an overhaul of how you do business and you're overwhelmed. Maybe it's in a relationship (or series of them). Maybe it's in your body or mind (lack of health, balance, confidence, mental unrest). Maybe it's at work (stress, lack of promotion, mediocre results). Maybe it's showing up in the people or organization you manage, where change is required but is being resisted for one reason or another. Any way you slice it, you want things to be different but you're just not sure how to make that happen. So, like the brilliant person that you are, you invited me to offer the solution and I'm here to deliver it.

You've already wasted countless hours, days, years, and maybe even decades on that nonsense. Stop it. Stop it right now. You can't stop it "back then" and you really can't afford to waste another precious moment. You can't reclaim the past so please don't waste your now thinking about your "back then." Please don't put it off for "someday" when you'll get it all together. You're in the right now, so do it right now. You don't have to waste any more time. That's the good news. Knowing that you have fleeting moments in this lifetime makes every decision that much easier to make because you're making each decision based on an appreciation for life's brevity and the inconsequential nature of most things we concern ourselves with. Once you make up your mind that you're done with all that nonsense, you can choose how you think and therefore decide differently how you'll behave. As Dr. Seuss so eloquently stated:

"Congratulations! Today is your day. You're off to Great Places! You're off and away! You have brains in your head. You have feet in your shoes. You can steer yourself any direction you choose."

~ Promises, Promises, Promises ~

"It is in our darkest moments
that we must focus to see the light." ~Aristotle

So, what can you look forward to learning in this book? In my world, I'm a huge proponent of setting intentions before you start anything, even a trip to the grocery store. What do I mean by "intentions?" Intentions are what we hope to gain or give in an experience. These intentions are best when they are limited by what we can control or influence. For example, if I'm going into a potentially tough meeting with a client, my intention would not be "to see Bob Client happy." I suppose I could, but then I'd be more focused on him and his experience than perhaps what I could do to control my inputs and influence the process.

A better intention would be "to remain calm and positive and to create an environment for change." Whatever the words may be, your intention is your North Star. It's the focal point that draws you toward it, making decisions about what to say and how to behave in order to make it come true. To manifest *what you want* into *what you have.* It's such a simple and easy practice and well worth the effort. You'll learn more about it later in this book, but I couldn't go on without a quick overview as I present my own intentions. They are to:

- Give you a roadmap for change, so you can finally get unstuck.
- Offer a roadmap for change for your team or company so you can succeed.
- Show you that you are writing the story of your life, either actively and proactively or passively.
- Provide a way for you to get your needs met by changing the way you think, feel, and behave.
- Vastly improve your emotional agility and the degree to which you can master change.
- Teach you to embrace what you can control, influence....and everything else...and in so doing, balance conviction with acceptance.
- Demonstrate how you can move along your spectrum of qualities toward being the person you want to be, seeing that whatever you're doing now is just a different manifestation of or degree to which you really want to behave.

In effect, my intentions are now our agreements for what I've promised to deliver. I've shared them openly so you know where I'm headed, where my North Star is located. This list tells you what you can expect to gain from the book and how best to use it in your life. I want you to seek these things as you read the book and do the exercises. I want you to challenge your own understanding and experience of things so that you can receive all of these gifts I'm offering, with some work required on your part. For those of you who have heard me speak you know that my purpose in writing and speaking about these practices is to raise consciousness and awareness and increase growth and discourse.

After I spend some pages discussing this concept of Emotional Agility, the remaining chapters are a discussion of the change process itself and its interface with Emotional Agility.

The five-step change process looks like this:

Step 1: Awareness
Step 2: Acceptance
Step 3: Assessment
Step 4: Action
Step 5: Adjustment

It's not complicated. Honestly, it's pretty intuitive. And, it's easy to commit to memory so you can quickly identify where you are and where you need to go. You'll find down-to-earth explanations, examples, and exercises to provide you with the tools necessary to change one little thing in your life...or the entire canvas. I won't tell you that any of this is going to be a cakewalk, but if you need that, just lay back and let the rest of your life happen to you. Because, so sorry, but I can't help you if you won't put in the effort. Unless, of course, you recognize that you're "lazy" and that's the thing you want to change. That I can help with, so let's give it a whirl.

Shall we get started? If you're ready, hurry it up and turn the page. Well, read this quote first...

"It took me quite a long time to develop a voice, and now that I have it, I am not going to be silent." ~ Madeline Albright

EMOTIONAL AGILITY

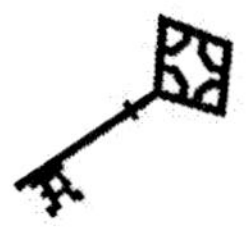

"If you do not like where you are, then change it.
You are not a tree."~ Author Unknown

This book is grounded in one key principle: In order to change your life you have to change your behavior, and behavior follows feelings and feelings follow thoughts. The motivation to change may come from a variety of sources, broken into *sticks* (the negative things that push you to make changes so you can avoid them) and *carrots* (the positive rewards that pull you to make changes so you can acquire them). As Freud told us, we human beings seek to avoid pain (sticks) and increase pleasure (carrots). What are these sticks and carrots?

Sticks: Failed relationships, business losses, physical maladies
Carrots: Healthy relationships, being an effective employee/leader, happiness, less stress

From that premise, this book creates a model of two things:

1. *Emotional agility* (what you can do to be stronger, healthier, etc. through emotional and relational agility).
2. How to **increase** your *emotional agility.*

Agility means to move quickly and easily with sharpness of skill. Corporations are replete with "agile" method interventions to assist them in adapting to and responding to changing environments and demands. Having *Emotional Agility* means being conditioned to use strategies, thought shifts, and emotional management to address stressors and conflict with comfort, ease, confidence, and clarity.

Agility equals high emotional competence mixed with high change-ability.

Emotional Agility answers the burning question of how change occurs: Through mastering emotional agility. How do you get agile?

- Learn strategies
- Develop thought shifts
- Open your mind to new alternatives
- Practice doing things differently

Agility is enhanced through stretching training, practice, and awareness, much like you would become more agile in playing a sport: Through flexibility, strength, and endurance. The more you practice, the better you get. It's as simple as that. Plus, the more you practice, the more options you're likely to try so the more options you have for the next time around. What do I mean by "options?"

Let's say you've been the "messy" person for the greater portion of your life. You'd like to change that so you're reading this book so you can make that happen. The first thing you might do is to change your thoughts about yourself being "messy." Maybe you'll entertain the thought that you are sometimes messy and sometimes you keep order. I used to work as a professional organizer and one of my clients had a house that was chaotic, messy, cluttered, and overwhelming.

All except her bathroom. Her bathroom was ordered and neat. We built her habits for the rest of the house from what worked for her in the bathroom. I've found that most people have a "bathroom;" a corner in their lives that works, even when the rest of it isn't. Find your "bathroom" and find your floorplan for strength and change. Need help identifying it? Here are some questions to guide you:

What is the thing that you're trying to "fix" about yourself?

Is there a place in your life where you display that positive quality or behavior, even a little? Describe it here.

What is it about that place (relationship, circumstance) that brings that out in you? Why there and not in other places?

Now that you know that you *can* do that, it's time TO do that. Let this book be your guide to stretching out, toning up, and gearing up for the life you've imagined.

"We all have dreams. But in order to make dreams come into reality, it takes an awful lot of determination, dedication, self-discipline, and effort." ~ Jesse Owens

~ Emotional Barometer ~

Everyone (aside from sociopaths and a few other personality disorders) have an emotional barometer. Your emotional barometer measures pressure and stress and allows for a prediction of a short-term change in the emotional environment. When your emotional barometer is working, you can see things coming. If you can accurately gauge the reading on your emotional barometer, you are better equipped to be emotionally agile. If you know that bad weather is predicted, you can gather the resources to ride it out. If stress and pressure take you by surprise, even maximum agility may leave you stressed out. Being in tune to emerging stress and the influence of others helps you to be more effective, not because you can change others, but because you can be less reactive and more deliberate in your responses to their actions and the onset of stress.

~ Breaking Down Emotional Agility ~

Recognize that you have 360 degrees of options. That's an amazing number of choices, most of which you've never even considered. I can't tell you how many people come to me and tell me that they "have" to do such and such or they "have no choice." Bull. There is an entire sea full of options in front of you, every minute of every day. The more agile you are, the more options you can *see* and *employ*. Emotional agility is demonstrated by embracing and enacting choice over thoughts, feelings, and actions. Your degree of Emotional Agility is measured by the *ease* and *flexibility* of embracing and enacting that choice. Emotional Agility is change in and of itself: It allows for it by its nature. In other words, it's being flexible.

The hallmarks of Emotional Agility are:

1. **Insight** – Understanding people and oneself, seeing motivations, aware of stuff beyond the "chatter" or "noise" of what the problem may look like on the outside.

2. **Distance-ability** – Decreasing emotional and reactive response by being able to create distance and perspective about the situation.

3. **Flexibility** – Thinking and behaving differently in response to internal and external cues.

How do you know when you have a high degree of *insight*? You'll be able to focus on the thoughts, feelings, and actions of others and not just your own. You'll be inclined to look first at the motivations behind a person's behavior instead of "they did such and such." Most importantly, your focus will be on understanding the problem instead of jumping to conclusions that lead you straight to blame others.

How do you know when you're a pro at *distance-ability*? You won't react to the behavior of others without thinking it through first. You'll tend to be calm, even in the most reactive and volatile situations. You'll be able to observe how the situation wants you to feel, but you won't fall into that trap without calculating the consequences.

How do you know when you're mastering *flexibility*? You'll note that you have a variety of options in any given situation. You recognize that even though you might instinctively want to act in a certain way, you *do* have other options you can consider. You observe internal and external cues that might affect the way you think and behave and use these cues to make decisions about how to respond.

It's now time to rate yourself on the three hallmarks of Emotional Agility. Using the descriptions above, describe in the spaces below how you think you're doing on each component. Remember to be critical so you can identify the gaps you need to close.

How are you doing being insightful? Is it a hit or miss thing or are you known for your insight?

How are you doing using your distance-ability? Are there certain triggers you struggle with more than others?

How are you doing with your flexibility? Can you see your options but actually thinking or behaving with the "same" situation (versus with a new approach) proves challenging?

"Give a man a fish and you feed him for a day;
teach a man to fish and you feed him for a lifetime." ~Maimonides

I want to help you to change every little and big thing about you that drives you nuts and holds you back from the life you could be the living and the success you (and your company) could be enjoying. I could write volumes tackling each possible issue my readers may have. I offer examples throughout the book to help you address particular habits that people struggle with, but my focal point is on helping you to develop Emotional Agility , not on every possible habit.

When you develop Emotional Agility, you inherently make yourself open to and capable of change. Then, you can decide which changes you want to make. You develop emotional competence (awareness, reflective thought, tactics and strategies, analysis) and "grey zone" thinking, which opens you up to change as you see fit. Like stretching and doing strength training and endurance activities, you can decide from there if you want to ride a bike for a distance, run, swim, etc. You've conditioned your body for a wide variety of activities so you get to choose how to apply your flexibility, strength, and endurance. The Agility Matrix depicts Emotional Agility: **How thoughts, feelings, and behaviors are influenced by and influence circumstances and choices.**

Three things that you need to know about the Agility Matrix:

1. The Agility Matrix is neither voodoo nor rocket science.
2. The Agility Matrix amounts to control that is exercised in healthy and productive ways.
3. The Agility Matrix is built on intuitive thinking, about how things come to be in our lives.

~ Agility Matrix ~

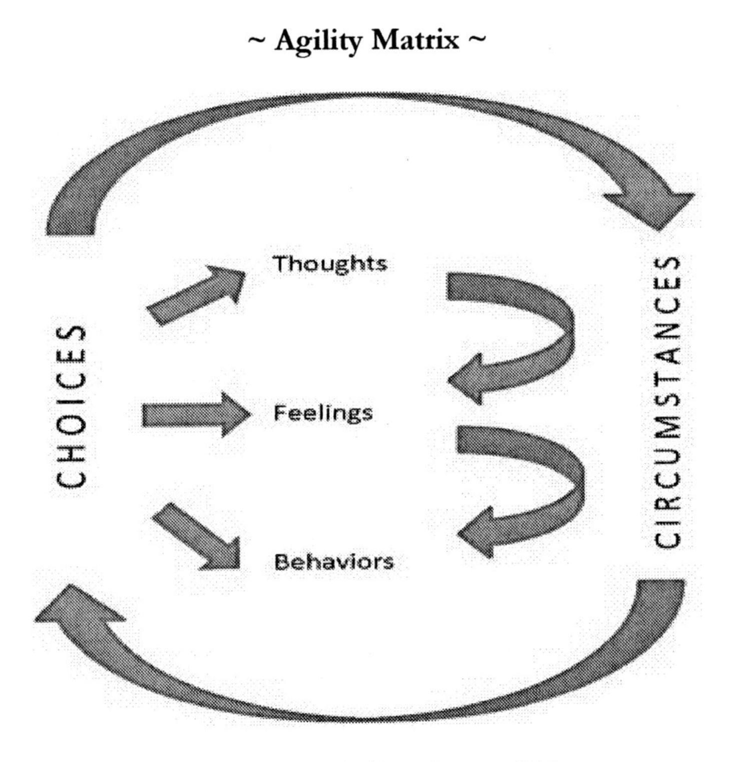

Property of Dr. Bridget Cooper, 2015

When I was in school, it drove me nuts when I'd see a diagram and then below it was a page of text trying to explain it to me in some complicated fashion. It made me feel like I was expected to channel Aristotle or Einstein. I'm not going to torment you that way, at least not on this page. Below is the nitty gritty of the model, in easy-to-read bullet form. The pathway looks like this:

- We make choices about how to think about things.
- Our thoughts about things lead to our feelings about things.
- Our feelings about things lead to how we behave in response to things.
- How we behave leads to a host of circumstances in our lives.
- Those circumstances then influence the choices we have and the ones we make.

The matrix feeds backwards, as well:

- The circumstances in our lives affect how we think about things.
- How we think about those circumstances in our lives affects our feelings.
- Those feelings affect our behavior.
- Our (thoughts and feelings and) behavior then affects the choices we make about things in our lives.

I need to mention the nasty "c" word here before we proceed: Control. Oh, it's not nasty because we don't like it. No, no, no. We LOVE it. We are often downright obsessed with it. It's nasty because we allow the drive for it to take over our lives, to our detriment and sometimes even our death. The point is driven home in my book, *Feed The Need* (2014), because control is one of the four core human needs. (If you want to learn more about it and the other three needs, order it up via my website, www.piecesinplace.com).

We want it, a lot of it. Some of us are obvious about it. Some of us cloak our desire for it under the guise of being "helpful" or "caring." Don't kid yourself: You love having control, often over circumstances and people. It's okay. It really is. It's natural. Control makes us feel safer. For those of you who read *Feed The Need* already, remember this?

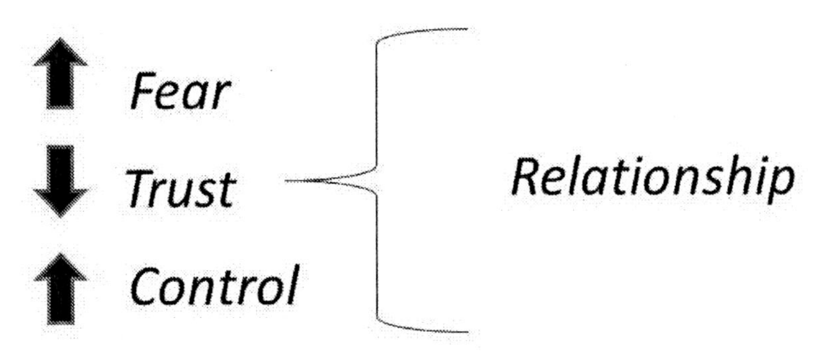

Basically, what this model illustrates is that when we feel fear (anxiety, uncertainty), we don't trust (ourselves, other people, circumstances) and we want to exert control (effective or ineffective). Sometimes this control is suitably placed (we focus ourselves and what we can do to mitigate the fear or build trust in the relationship or situation). Sometimes it is mistakenly placed on the uncontrollable: Other people or circumstances. The latter makes us certifiably crazy but that usually doesn't stop us. Oh, no. That usually makes us *more* hell bent on exerting *more* effort on trying to "fix" the situation. Xanax (or Jack Daniels), here we come!

"Please tell us, Bridget, that you have an alternative!"

I'm so glad you said that, because I do!

It's a simple concept, really, but one that will keep you out of the funny farm and perhaps even wean you off the psychotropic drugs that have kept a complete psychotic episode at bay. I call it the Control Buckets. It looks like this (in my head, anyway):

~ Bring Me A Bucket! ~

As much as we'd like to control everything and everyone, it's just not possible. There are three groupings of things in the world which I've broken down into your "Control Buckets."

The first teeny weeny, teensy tiny bucket is what you can control. Now, in this bucket are your thoughts, feelings, and behaviors. It's things like your attitude and your boundaries, and what you spend your time and your money on.

The next itsy bit bigger bucket is what you can influence. In this bucket are the thoughts, feelings, and behaviors of others. Wait…what? Am I saying that you are in charge of how other people think, feel, and act? Heck to the no! I'm simply saying that we are all playing a beautiful game of bumper cars out there in the big world of ours. You can affect how others feel in relationship with you (to some extent). You can affect how other people think, by writing books like yours truly.

Then there is the enormous bucket that covers the rest of the landscape. And what comprises that big ol' bucket? It's everything you cannot control. This includes other people and what they actually do, circumstances, events, and the passage of time (and death and taxes and…you get my drift). Sounds easy enough. If it's so easy, why are people stuck in a dysfunctional pattern of exercising ineffective control?

Confusion. I haven't yet had a client who hasn't struggled with control. They get their buckets all wrong and focus their efforts on trying to control things that they can't possibly control. They put their hands in other people's buckets, which usually leads to their own buckets being violated. Invariably, they get completely stressed out trying to exert control over circumstances and people that won't acquiesce to their demands. But that doesn't stop them from trying, and exhausting themselves in the process. Sound familiar?

Recently there was a tremendous traffic jam on an interstate highway just up the road from my house. The traffic abruptly stopped in its tracks. For three hours. Three HOURS. No one moved, not even an inch. A friend of mine was stuck in this mess and we used the internet to investigate what was going on and how long we thought it might take to clear up. We wanted to know if this was a temporary snag or if he should get comfy and settle in for the night. I wasn't even on the highway and I was trying to exert some control via information gathering. To be fair, we were supposed to be on a date that night so I did have a pony in that race.

Nevertheless, we knew that we weren't in control of how fast that traffic jam was going to ease up. The only thing we could control was our response to it; whether we found reasons to laugh or scream. I found a website where people could investigate and post about traffic issues and accidents and I was amused by the spectrum of responses. Some were raging at the incident, hell bent on exacting revenge on the people blocking the breakdown lane, the slow-moving police who could address the situation differently, and so on.

Then there was Bubba. I'm not sure if it was a screen name or his real name; I suppose it doesn't matter. But God bless Bubba. This guy was a breath of fresh air. Imagine how many ways people sitting in this jam for hours were inconvenienced. Imagine how uncomfortable they were. Imagine how much they needed to visit the bathroom. Imagine how hungry and thirsty they were. Imagine how much they wanted to be anywhere but there, in their cars, scene unchanging, with no hope in sight of getting to where they wanted and needed to be.

What did Bubba offer? Humor. He bragged about sitting on his cozy couch, watching the game, eating delicious Chinese food, and having a relaxing beverage. He bantered with the other post contributors, bringing a smile to their faces, no doubt, making the time spent a little easier to bear.

Consider for a moment how many people who were stuck in that unbelievable jam were able to conjure up a smile or a laugh? How many of them got out of their cars and met a new friend in the highway-turned-parking-lot? And, how many look back on that night with some level of amusement and gratitude? Unfortunately, probably not many, which is so unfortunate. Think about it: It was three (or more) hours of their lives that they'll never get back. They had no control over the events, yet a great number of them brought thoughts and feelings of anger and disdain into their present (and future).

Not Bubba. Now, my guess is that Bubba was in that traffic jam, too, and just decided to bring some levity to the moment. He used his imagination to bring him where he wanted to be but wasn't: Home, fed, hydrated, and comfortable. For those on that online thread, he brightened their night, too. Well, some of them. Because there were some who sailed right past his contribution and posted their rage at the situation and frustration with their fellow man.

Bubba, on the other hand, tried to share his happy with everyone who would listen. Someday I'd like to meet Bubba so we can discuss the Agility Matrix because he seems to understand it and live it. No one in that traffic jam, regardless of their level of frustration, could have affected the outcome. They could have, however, completely shaped how they spent that time behind the wheel. They could have called a friend they hadn't spoken with a while and caught up, without distraction. They could have gotten out of their car and met a new friend. They could have gotten a few things done on their "to-do" list, or write one down. They could have shared stories and sung songs and made up games with their passengers. Or, they could be Bubba.

I'm inviting you to be the Bubba in your own life. To focus on controlling the things that you can: Your thoughts, feelings, and behaviors. Your choices and responses to circumstances, too. Focus on influencing the things you can influence. Seek to improve the thoughts and feelings others have when they come into contact with you. In essence, for the sake of all things good in this world, own and live the Agility Matrix. Observe how it comes alive in your life. See how the choices you make affect, and are affected by, your thoughts, feelings, and behaviors. Witness how those choices (and your thoughts, feelings, and behaviors) create circumstances in your life that either benefit or threaten to destroy you.

Being a master of the Agility Matrix also requires that you acknowledge how you perceive and respond to (via your thoughts, feelings, and behaviors) circumstances. Through your state of mind, you manifest what you have and what you experience. Despite your most valiant efforts to the contrary, you're not in charge of other people or circumstances. Ever. You might influence them, and you might even convince yourself that you've got "things" under control.

Believe me when I tell you that it's an illusion. You've done all that you can do to control things that you can control and influence the things that you can influence, but the only person or entity you have any chance of controlling is you. Just you. Big, bad, beautiful, complicated, impressive, crazy, wonderful you. You can control no one and nothing else. Focusing on you is a full-time job. Getting your thoughts lined up consistent with what is best for you, those you love, and the world around you is no simple task. Supporting and indulging feelings consistent with those thoughts, well, Hercules had lighter loads. Acting on those feelings in a healthy and constructive manner is another bridge to cross.

Why in the world do you think you have time or energy left over to chase down other people (and their thoughts, feelings, and behaviors) and circumstances (many of which are led by chance and chaos)? Safety and control are to blame. We, as humans, have a core need to feel safe. Makes sense: We don't want to die and a lack of safety can equal death. In order to feel safe, we need to control as many variables as possible. Because our eyes face outward, we are often drawn to look outside of ourselves for solutions to our feelings of fear and lack of safety. Control reduces fear. Feeling in control makes us feel safer and less fearful. So, we seek control in any way we can.

Anyone who has ever attended one of my workshops across the country has most likely heard me pose this question: When you witness someone (including you) trying to control things, instead of seeing this person as a controlling jerk, can you instead try to observe why they might be holding fear in their hearts? I've never known of a situation where a person who was trying to control more than their own thoughts, behaviors, and actions wasn't wrestling with fear. Some people call this fear "anxiety." In certain people and situations, fear comes out as a "more acceptable" emotion: Anger. This has some gender bias in it, but I've found that women generally have an easier time expressing fear (versus anger) than men. For women, it often comes out as anxiousness and even anxiety disorders. When it rears its ugly head as anger, it can show up as hostility, rage, and coldness (distance).

You've met people riddled with anxiety. What is the number one thing that they seek? Control. Not just control limited to their own person (thoughts, feelings, behaviors) but other people and things. Their anxiety stems from a reality that most of us find hard to swallow: That we are not in control of anything but ourselves, and even that's sporadic. Anxious people have to face that head on every minute of every day. Their successful treatment focuses their attention on their span of control (what they can control). In a sense, those with diagnosed anxiety disorders may have a leg up on the rest of us since they are being exposed to the Agility Matrix and their livelihood depends on grasping and living its tenets.

In order to effectively manage their anxiety they need to come to terms with what they can control and what they can't. What they can influence and what they can't. They have to manage those elements that they can control and influence and learn to let go of the rest. And "the rest" is a huge landscape. It's like Bubba's traffic jam. People died that day and traffic didn't move for many hours. And there was no way off that highway. There was nothing to do but wait. The only thing those poor drivers could do while they waited was control their thoughts, feelings, and actions. They could make the most of a bad situation by letting go of what they couldn't control (the traffic jam) and focus on what they could (their attitude about it). Imagine if a sizeable number let the lack of control get to them? There could have been mayhem. A riot could have broken out, particularly involving the people who parked their cars in the breakdown lane. Luckily that didn't happen, but we've all seen media coverage of times when tempers flared and bad things occurred.

~ The Domino Effect of Anger ~

"The tragedy of life is not death,
but what we let die inside of us while we live." ~ Norman Cousins

When your need for control isn't met, you are apt to get pretty angry. People are often windows and not mirrors. Hurt people hurt people. When we are in pain or disgruntled with our lives, we are apt to strike out, hitting whatever is on our path. Sometimes it's complete strangers. Often it's the people closest to us.

When my mom died suddenly last year, I was reminded of this human pattern. I had just gotten off of a contentious phone call with my big sister (who was insisting on acting like a classic big sister in my mother's affairs, taking charge and being just as condescending toward me as you can imagine) and a credit card company called me. It was a recording (which I find irritating under the best of circumstances) and after pressing several buttons to get to a real person, a man answered and proceeded to take a similar tone with me that my sister just had.

Poor guy. He didn't see what was coming his way as I knocked that angry ball right back at him, leveling him and his company with my disgust at how they were charging me a ridiculous late fee when my balance was paid in full. Bottom line: They were technically right about the fee but I had taken enough slander that morning to fill me up so I wasn't anywhere near the point of graciously accepting responsibility for my oversight.

No *way*. After he cut me with his own sharp tongue and attitude (which, by the way, I don't recommend and I conduct training and provide tools to rise above this sort of customer service nightmare situation), I realized that all I wanted was to shut the world out and crawl into a hole and grieve my many losses over what was a very tough year in my life. His arrogance was sending me through the roof. Let's just say that a rooftop was *not* where I needed to be. I needed a shift. A way out of this angry, resentful, shamed, shunned, minimized place. I was a cactus needing a hug.

Well, since I did write a book about needs and getting them met, I figured I'd better get busy making that happen. So I did. I got off the phone and I reached out to a friend. I vented. I snuggled. I received validation for my plight. What happened next? I started to feel better. I shifted. I shifted away from anger and fear toward love and acceptance. To understanding: myself and others. I experienced in real time that hurt people really do hurt people. I was hurt so I was lashing out. I had decided that I was not going to strike back at my sister because she was incapable of receiving the truth or welcoming real growth through any pain I might send her way. She was likely only to throw it back harder, causing more psychic damage to her and to me in the process, and polluting the space in the universe that exists between us.

That was not the energy I wanted to be responsible for creating, or multiplying. Instead, I struck out at a stranger, someone who I'd never have to see or hear from again. Not that this was a good thing: He likely left our conversation irritated and growling at the next person who came into his space. From there it probably kept going and going. So, my little tantrum possibly led to a crappy day for countless people. Yuck.

I sat and contemplated that for a while, wishing that I'd completed my "shift" (and gotten my snuggle and empathy) *before* I'd answered the phone. Without reading one more line further I'll bet that you can figure out my advice: Don't pick up the phone or answer the door or head to another appointment before you shift back to a calm, loving center and let go of the nasty juice you just drank before you wreak havoc on the world. Yeah, you. Wreaking all sorts of vile destruction on the world with your hurt self. You know you do it. If you say that you don't *ever* do that, well then, you probably should skip to the next section or just go write a book yourself on how to move through life without denting anyone's spirit. We need a whole legion of people like you so go forth and multiply. Please.

Assuming you're human, what can you learn from my meltdown? Check your intentions. Ask yourself what you're looking to get from an interaction. To harm? To share pain? Or to ease it? Remember, people are not necessarily mirrors to *you* but their actions are clearly windows into *them*. Mother Theresa could have had people who treated her badly. That's a window to someone else's soul, not a mirror to yours, unless you tolerate their behavior. Then that's *all* you.

When you choose people to come into your life they are a mirror of your CHOICE, not necessarily of your inner humanity. They mirror what you think you deserve to have in your realm and what you think serves you. I'm speaking, of course, of the people that you choose to have in your life, not those thrust upon you by circumstance (like family and co-workers and strangers you meet in passing or through loved ones.) Your behavior is a window into *you*. Who *you* are and where *you're* at. Their behavior is window into *them*; who *they* are and where *they're* at.

The optimal goal of practicing emotional agility is to become a ninja. An emotional, relationship ninja. Not the fighting type of ninja, but possessing quiet, calm, clarity, and peace in knowing what you are focused on and aiming your energy toward.

"Believe you can and
you're halfway there." ~ Theodore Roosevelt

~ Stuck U. ~

I haven't met a person who doesn't know what stuck feels like. I've actually met some people who forget what *not* being stuck feels like. If that's you, you've felt trapped, burdened, and encumbered for so long you've lost sight of what freedom from it feels like. Even if you haven't been stuck forever it can sure feel like it. You're frustrated and you want to be anywhere but where you are but you can't see the path out. You've focused on what you've been doing wrong (or what's been "going" wrong) to the point where you're struggling to see anything ever being different.

Maybe you're fat or out of shape and the simple task of getting dressed in the morning is making you miserable (been there, done that). Perhaps you're so filled with hate and resentment for someone (or some circumstance or just the world in general) that you're physically and mentally sick. Or, you're overwhelmed by the people and things around you because you've been swallowing up their nonsense and drama like it's candy for far too long. It could be that you're in the same dead-end job and it's literally sucking the life out of you. Maybe your company initiates changes but then you find yourselves right back in the same old spot like a bad case of déjà vu. Your company has been engaging in change for change's sake but your performance is flat-lining. Bottom line: You're stuck and you need relief. Ready for a different course?

~ Agile U. ~

"When you're in peace, it's a place of power." ~ Joel Osteen

What do agile people, groups, companies look like? Agile people are consistently and constantly assessing their competence, shifting course if new information or relevant feedback is acquired. They focus on quickly-changing realities. They don't wait for dramatic conclusion; they adapt as things are moving. They do what works for them, not necessarily what "experts" advise. They roll with the punches. They go with their ideas and their gut. They think for themselves. They monitor progress and evaluate their own work. They work to develop their frontal cortex, and succeed and fail on their own terms.

According to Jim Collins (author of *Good to Great*, 2001), great companies stimulate progress while staying true to their mission. Agile entities seek constant improvement and are shown an immediate (or nearly so) and flexible response to change. They take responsibility for their own action and focus on the immediate future. They don't get weighed down by "someday" fears by dealing with what is in right front of them. Agile people and companies are not perfect by any stretch. They have problems. Problems come, but then problems go. It's not a problem-free existence, but things don't linger for long. Weight that comes on, comes back off. Constructive feedback is solicited and incorporated into new thought and behavior patterns, visible to the outside observer. Change is felt within, and when change is needed a plan is created and followed. Challenges are temporary because with challenge comes response. Promotions or job changes aren't elusive, at least not for long. Feedback is not only welcomed, but sought after, so that effectiveness and productivity can be maximized.

An organization with emotional agility seeks out change. Emotionally agile companies seek continuous improvement and they don't back down from conflict or issues in their organization. They don't pretend to be in a better position than they are, valuing honest assessment. They aren't bullies, but they don't let issues fester and eat at the fabric of their culture. They construct and empower feedback loops, seeking out new insights and suggestions for the betterment of the organization. They don't respond erratically to challenges or change; they are thoughtful and intentional. They put these insights into action, and monitor the plan.

Now, I must make a critical point here as it relates to "agility." You cannot, and I repeat, you cannot consider yourself agile just because you moved from one relationship or job to another. Movement itself is not "agility." It's just movement. In the case of romantic relationships, moving from one bed to another usually indicates that you haven't done the work on you before you bring your "polluted" you into the next relationship. Job hopping is the same. To be considered emotionally agile you need to own what's yours and give credit for what's not. Maybe you don't have that conversation with your former partner, maybe you do. If you don't complete this assessment step you're hiding that mess from your next partner, steeped deep in the waters of denial.

We all know that seeing things in black and white makes exits easier. If your partner or boss is evil incarnate it's easier to jet. Grey has to be waded through and reckoned with. When it's "clear," you can clap your hands and hail, "hallelujah!" When it's grey, you may linger. I am not, at any level, advocating that if you're in an unsafe (physically or emotionally) space that you hang around until you can make your way out of the grey. If that is the case, I am advocating that you take a few (thousand) deep breaths after you leave to acknowledge that nothing is purely black and white. As a friend of mine said, "even Hitler had birthday parties." And that guy is evil incarnate. Elizabeth Gilbert went through two countries and a whole heck of a lot of soul searching before she was clear-headed enough to enter into her next relationship. Do yourself a favor: Take the Elizabeth Gilbert approach, minus the world travels if that doesn't fit your capabilities.

Is Emotional Agility another name for Emotional Intelligence? No, but they are related, so let's discuss the connections and the disparities so we can be clear on the concepts and how to apply them.

"All learning has an emotional base." ~ Plato

~ Emotional Intelligence: Backdrop ~

Before we start talking about emotional intelligence, let's first pay homage to the thought leaders that brought the term to our public consciousness. Tracing back to the 1930s, Edward Thorndike described the concept of "social intelligence," measuring a person's ability to get along well with others. In the 1940s, David Wechsler proposed that emotional regulation has a direct link to being successful in life. The focus on emotional strength continued with Abraham Maslow's work in the 1950s. Then, in 1975, Howard Gardner introduced the concept of multiple intelligences that affect a person's competency in the world. Wayne Payne, a doctoral student, introduced the term "emotional intelligence" in his doctoral dissertation in 1985. An article by that same name was published by Peter Salovey and John Mayer (1990) whose names have since become synonymous with "emotional intelligence."

Daniel Goleman brought worldwide attention to the emotional intelligence landscape with the immensely popular book, "Emotional Intelligence: Why It Can Matter More Than IQ" (1995), solidifying the concept into popular culture. Goleman capitalized on the 1990s surge in passion for leadership tomes to provide intuitive guidance on how to lead companies and organizations through challenge and change. He posited that emotional intelligence is a set of competencies that includes: Self-awareness, self-regulation, social skill, empathy, and motivation. It's been studied a great deal and has shown to affect bullying behavior (initiating and tolerating it), self-esteem, drug-use avoidance, job success, mental and physical health, life satisfaction, and leadership effectiveness.

In summary, emotional intelligence refers to the ability to perceive, use, understand, and manage emotions. Can it be learned or are you born with it? Researchers don't agree on the answer to that. I contend that it's a blend of nature and nurture. I have found in my work with people anecdotally that you are born with emotional intelligence potential that you either work or let atrophy. Your upbringing and the people and circumstances that you surround yourself with will serve to maximize (or truncate) your emotional intelligence. You may be born with a higher innate level of it than another person, but you can throw it away just as easy as a bad sandwich. On the other hand, you can be born with a limited amount of it and have all sorts of impediments thrown in front of you and you can seek and build it in yourself, and end up as an emotional intelligence master. You want that? You're going to have to work for it, even if you were born with high potential. You don't make the Olympics sitting on your couch. And that marathon isn't going to finish itself.

How does Emotional Agility differ from Emotional Intelligence?

- Both have competencies that can be learned.
- Emotional Agility features insight, distance-ability, and flexibility.
- Emotional Intelligence features self-awareness (like insight), self-regulation, social skill, empathy, and motivation.
- You can be emotionally agile and not emotionally intelligent, though that is rare.
- You can be emotionally intelligent but not emotionally agile, and this is frequent.

In essence, Emotional Agility stresses *mastery of perspective* and *responsiveness to adaptation and change.* Over time and experience, our emotional intelligence and emotional agility may be stunted or may grow. With the help of this book, you will be able to grow your emotional agility, assuring your ability to adapt and change as it serves you to do so. Being both emotionally intelligent and emotionally agile serves you well.

~ Concluding Thoughts ~

Emotional Agility is a set of tactics, but it is not being cold and emotionless. It's not being unconcerned or without passion. On the contrary, it's being passionate about being capable to respond, not react. Or, to react only when necessary, like in times of immediate danger. Even then, it's better to respond, to be conditioned to stay calm in the face of daunting circumstances. That's what I mean by fearless. Just doing things. Not hesitating. Not saying no all the time. Not being paralyzed.

This book is built with the intention to maximize your emotional intelligence by providing new frameworks, approaches, tactics, and tools. It serves as "emotional intelligence boot camp," so start stretching, get some comfy clothes on, and lace up your sneakers: It's time to smarten the heck up and unstick yourself like only *you* can.

As you progress through this book, please remember this important strategy: Don't focus on breaking an old pattern or habit. Replace it with a new one. Focus on the new, on your target, not on where you've just left. Your neck will strain if you keep looking back, and you're bound to bump into something.

Life isn't perfect. Life is messy. Emotional Agility helps us to keep perspective when we're riding the top of the wave and/or crashing upon the shore. Instead of operating to survive, how would it feel to operate to succeed? If you want that, focus on resilience. Change is constant. New challenges await. Those who find their greatness first had to navigate through some storms. Be flexible enough to try new approaches. This book is your key out…are you going to turn it?

Key Chapter Concepts

- Changing your situation means you must change your behavior.
- Emotional Agility = High emotional competence and high change-ability. 3 Pieces: Insight, Distance-ability, Flexibility.
- Agility Matrix shows that we have Choices about our Thoughts, Feelings, & Behaviors. Those create our Circumstances, which then affect our Choices.
- We have three Control Buckets which need to be used properly.

"You can't wait for inspiration.
You have to go after it with a club." ~ Jack London

4

AWARENESS

We are our choices." ~ Jean Paul Sartre

Whoever told you that growth was fun was out of their ever-loving mind. Sure, I can paint it sparkly and bright for you and talk all about the sunny side of the new life you're creating but that's only part of the story. Growth comes with (sometimes) cataclysmic pain. What's that? You can't wait to get going on this path of growth I'm offering? Well, you sick puppy you, let's get this party started.

Reaching awareness is the first, and often most jarring, step in the change process. It requires that you wake up from your slumber and face the cold, hard facts that you've created a situation (or a life) that just isn't cutting it. You're unhappy or unfulfilled and you're slowly realizing that denying it isn't doing you (or anyone else) any favors. Well, maybe it's doing other people some favors. Misery loves company, you know. Staying stuck is doing all sorts of fabulous things for the other stuck and miserable people in your life. Moles don't like the light. Neither do bitter, stuck, ignorant, hateful people. Becoming aware of your stuck-ness is going to shine some unflattering, fluorescent lighting in the squinting eyeballs of some of the people in your world, for certain.

Are you going to continue to smother the light, remain in denial, and stay stuck to be loyal to them? If so, please do yourself a favor: Put this book down and press the "forget" button in the center of your forehead so that none of the awareness that is creeping into your consciousness has any effect on you. You didn't know that you have a "forget" button on your forehead? Boy, you're developing all *sorts* of awareness, aren't you? Lucky you! I mean, I'm so sorry to hear that. You might not be able to walk away from this book after all.

~ Chapter Intention ~

"Change is the only constant in life." ~ Heraclitus

In this chapter you'll discover what Awareness looks like and how you can use it to set the foundation for bringing about change in your life. What changes might be screaming for you to pay attention and start taking some action to address them? It could be your:

- Weight or health
- Job/career
- Stagnant or slipping corporate/departmental results
- Relationship status, satisfaction, or dynamic
- Standard of living

~ You Have the Key, Dummy ~

"When sleeping women wake, mountains move." ~ Chinese Proverb

You awake? Good. Please pause for a quick second and call to mind the reason you picked up this book in the first place. What was it that spoke to you? I know, I know, it's got a super-cool title and great cover art and the author is, well, amazing, but what was it about the topic that told you to buy it and start reading it? I'll bet a whole truckload of money it's because you have something in your life that is unsettling (personal, interpersonal, or professional) and you want it to change. You want IT to change. Yep, I said it. If you had it your way you'd find a magic wand buried in the spine of this book that you could use to change whatever the "it" is that is causing you frustration and disruption.

If you haven't noticed already, I pull no punches. I'm not here to sell you on a simple solution to what ails you. I'm not going to hide behind nuance and flowery words to say what I have to say to you. I offer the hard truth. Is there any other kind of truth? Nope, didn't think so. Here it comes, ready or not.

The "it" that is causing you frustration and disruption is YOU. There's no "it" that is going to change out there and make your life better. It's a fantasy and a delusion. The only thing that is able to make a difference in how you're living your life is you. YOU. This book is about changing YOU. About getting YOU unstuck.

I'm not in the market to sprinkle magic fairy dust on the person/people/circumstance/ailment and make it all better. If I was, I'd be touring the world in my private jet, working one day a year. As attractive as that may seem, I'd be completely unfulfilled because I'm a girl who embraces a challenge and life isn't amazing if it's too easy. That's why your CEO may have made this book required reading. 'Cause your CEO caught my drift and realizes that your CEO can't change you: YOU have to change you. Ball is in your court: Whatcha gonna do?

So, let's talk about Awareness and what it means for the change process and you developing this thing called Emotional Agility. Plainly, if you don't know it's broke, you can't fix it. When your car starts making that funny noise it's your alert to visit the mechanic.

Personal growth works the same way. When things aren't working out "right," it's a sign that it might be time to make some changes in your life. Truth be told, life naturally has ups and downs and just because you've hit a bump it doesn't mean that you need to do a personal overhaul.

Being at a crossroads is different. A crossroads is a place when you can continue to head in the direction that you've become accustomed to, OR, you can take a turn and change things up. When you're unaware of being stuck, you blow through those crossroads like a stop sign on a familiar back road. So, how *do* you know that you're stuck? When you're sick and tired of being sick and tired. And, when any one (or more) of these apply:

- You're in a job that isn't rewarding and you dread going to.
- You're in a relationship that you're more likely to complain about rather than celebrate.
- You're fat and/or unhealthy.
- You're addicted (substance, sex, gambling, work, food)
- You're angry, anxious, or sad more than you are joyful.
- Your work team reminds you of a bad high school drama series.
- You're looking for validation (or comfort) in all the "wrong" (ineffective) places.
- You're holding a grudge.
- You're having ugly deja vous …haven't you been here before?
- You're given a self-help book or directed to seek counseling or a treatment program.
- You've just completed your third divorce.

What applies to your situation? What is it that you're aware of that spurred you to pick up this book? What's your "why" for change?

That last one in that list is no joke. A client came into my mentor's office years back and when asked, "when did you become aware that you had a problem?" the client responded, "it was after my third divorce." THIRD divorce? Wow. That guy was just coming out of a very dark hole, where Awareness just hadn't shone its light. I hope you're not that guy. I hope you're getting to this point before your third divorce (or third lost job or…). When you become aware of the fact that some aspect of your life is demanding your attention you can set the change process in motion.

~ Going to BAT ~

Awareness is also a state of being that can be toned like a muscle. If you are open to change and growth, your subconscious will be more open to being aware of the signs and symptoms of the need for it. When you resist *change and growth*, you set yourself up to resist *awareness* since it pushes you to confront the change process. How do you go about toning this *awareness muscle*? It's easy. Ready to go to bat (**B-A-T**, to be precise)? Here's the three-step process:

BE. Be present. Awareness requires that you are in the moment you're in. Assess your five senses (What do you see? Feel? Smell? Hear?).

ASK. Make a habit of asking yourself check-in questions after every appointment/activity and at the end of each day (How did that go? How did I affect the outcome? What could I have done differently?).

TRY. Instead of selecting your "regular" menu item, try something new. Take a different route to a place you visit frequently. Sit in a different seat. Give a different response to "how are you?" Note your reactions. Does it feel uncomfortable to do this? What are you feeling?

Sound easy? Okay, it takes WORK, but the best things do. The first step – being present – is the hardest for most of us. We are pulled in so many directions and we have the attention spans of squirrels on crack cocaine. Being present takes focus and calm. Focus and calm are traits that are rewarded in a monastery, not in corporate America. The more we produce, the more we succeed. We are constantly "connected" and "on" with our modern technology. At what cost? The divorce rate is high, kids are on meds and in therapy, school violence is rampant, and stress-related disease and disorders are more common than smiles. There *has* to be a better way.

There is. It's choosing presence over frenzy. Choosing the right energy to hold. Being present doesn't mean that you can't be highly productive. On the contrary; when you practice presence you expand your capacity for productivity. You accomplish more with higher quality. A scattered mind is not a clear mind. Scattered minds do things in a scattered way. Clear minds do things in a clear way. Here's the rhetorical question you knew was coming: Which would you rather have?

~Welcome To Your Launch Pad~

"Winning is a habit.
Unfortunately, so is losing." ~ Vince Lombardi

How long did you go without even recognizing that there *was* a problem? Some of you spent a portion of your lives unaware that a problem existed and it wasn't until you lost your job or your marriage or your health that you started to pay attention. Even then, you might have spent the aftermath of those "failures" convinced that you were the victim. You might have denied that the problem might just be you. That you might have a role in what's happening. That your story of powerlessness might be flawed. That you may not be the victim at every turn. That you might have power to change something. And, that you might even entertain the thought that changing something about the way you do things might have a positive effect on your situation.

Similar to the 12-Step™ program, the first step is admitting you have a problem, and the extent to which you have and do not have power. Except in the case of the disease of addiction, you aren't completely powerless. But you aren't the Great and Powerful Oz either. In order to shift your life and get yourself unstuck you have some work ahead of you. Part of owning that personal power is knowing when you need to surrender.

Knowledge isn't power, it's what you do with it. You could reach this first, critical step to change your life and just stay here, drowning in your "inspiring" awareness that something is terribly wrong (or not gloriously right) in your world, doing nothing to actually change it. You could remain aware of your discomfort but stay stuck right there. What's the magic potion? You have to possess a desire to change and an inner motivation to move forward. It might not be pain propelling you forward. Instead, it might be the sense that you are out of balance or can't find your equilibrium. Any way you slice it, you have to want it. Really want it.

"Some changes look negative on the surface
but you will soon realize that space is being created in your life
for something new to emerge." ~ Eckhart Tolle

~ Denial Isn't Just a River In Egypt ~

I've been waiting for years to use that one in print. It says so much about our human condition and one of our premiere coping mechanisms: Denial. Reality is tough, at some times more than others.

Without denial we would probably all be using the rotating door at the funny farm. Like everything, I judge denial on a spectrum. Too much and you're delusional and living in a fantasy land that is likely ticking off everyone around you. Too little and you're bathing in so much truth that you've developed a nervous tic (or twelve) to compensate. Facing up to the full truth of our world and our lives is daunting, to say the least. There's pain, fear, and quite a bit of downright evil out there and if we faced it head on every day it would be overwhelming and likely paralyzing. Denial, or turning away from the light of truth, can serve a purpose when it comes in small doses.

We often use denial differently in different areas of our lives. For instance, we might be in full-on denial in a relationship but can see our work situation clear as day. We tend to use denial in places where the truth threatens us the most. Let's say you have a boss who is disrespectful almost to the point of sexual harassment. The problem is that you have the perfect work situation: You get to work from home three days a week, your pay is higher than the market average, and they just funded your master's degree program. You might notice his inappropriate behavior but you may also tend to shrug it off ("there he goes being BOB again"). See, if you faced it head on you would risk your job and all its benefits. Denial comes in handy so that you don't have to resolve the issue and risk the "resolution."

"The way we choose to see the world
creates the world we see." ~ Barry Neil Kaufman

~ Faker Pants ~

Some truths just can't be denied. They stare us down and knock us squarely between the eyes. A marriage that is dead and in deep trouble. A child who is acting strangely and whose grades and friendships are plummeting. A career that is going nowhere, fast. We see the problems and we know that they exist, yet we shove this awareness down deep. Kind of like "Fight Club™," the rule is that no one speaks of the problems. Anyone who notices them puts on a happy face and pretends nothing is wrong. "How are things with Jane?" "*Terrific!*" "How's your son doing?" "*Great!*" "How's the job?" "*Fine!*" Like putting lipstick on a pig, you haven't done anything to solve the problem but you want everyone else to see the pretty image you're projecting, not the nasty, smelly truth. You're aware of the problem so you're not in a state of denial, but you aren't prepared to do the heavy lifting to make any changes and you sure as heck aren't planning to address it openly. If no one knows about it then it diminishes its weight. Um, not really, but it's helping you sleep better at night. You're staying just as stuck as the poor schmuck who is living in fantasyland in a full state of denial. The only difference between you two: You know better. More awareness gives you more responsibility.

Speaking of awareness, to illustrate what awareness looks like, I'm now going to offer a few examples of things that you may need to be aware of in your process. These are some common experiences I've observed as people proceed through the change process. Some of them got stuck when they faced these doozies, so my hope is that you can learn from their mistakes.

~ Hurdle #1: Universe Trust Fund Babies ~

One of the triggers that has stalled my change process a whole host of times is bitterness. It's a bitterness that arises out of jealousy. What does jealousy have to do with change? You asked, so I'll tell you, but you might not like it. I know I don't. I make my living helping other people see themselves and others more clearly and guide them to take actions to make their lives better. In that process is an implied promise that their lives will get better. The flip side holds true, as well: If they don't change and grow, their lives won't get better. So, what's the problem? Isn't all of that true? Well, sort of. And therein lies the pickle, and by "pickle" I mean that other green thing called *jealousy.*

Do you have people in your life (or on the periphery) who seem to be stunted in their growth, they do mean things, and they have no interest in changing and being better people yet *they* are driving new cars, getting promotions, posting party and vacation photos on Facebook, and generally "living it up?" I'll be honest: That makes me cringe and entertain such envy that it makes my skin turn green. How can they be such a-holes and reap all sorts of "rewards" from the Universe? What's the point of pursuing growth and change and being a better person while these people just drift through life, leaving carnage in their wake, yet wake up with few worries and all sorts of benefits? Management can't see that they are dragging the whole division down, and then the guy gets *promoted*?! What's up with THAT?

I call these folks "Universe Trust Fund Babies" (UTFBs). They are just sailing along, doing whatever it is that emotionally-stunted people do, riding on the backs of those of us who are doing the heavy lifting, committed to making the world a better, more loving place. They don't work for it in the way that you and I do; it's just given to them. It's nothing short of infuriating if you let it get under your skin. I don't know about you, but I get all "No fair-sies! What about ME?" Yeah, that always goes so well and changes so much.

Actually, it *does* change so much. It changes your energy. It creates your reality. Your sense of reality changes your thoughts about things, including the "unfairness" of it and the "luckiness" of those icky people. Your thoughts form the platform for your feelings. Your feelings inspire your behavior. Your behavior creates all sorts of outcomes that make your life a product of those choices. As a result, in a few quick steps you just went from hating on irritating people to wrecking your life. Really? Yup, that's how that works.

Do you want them to not only get the "Universe Trust Fund Baby" life but *also* tear holes into yours? That's just wrong. The deciding factor is *you.* It starts with your awareness of your bitterness and that this bitterness may be serving as a wall between you and the changes you want in your life. Don't let these UTFBs distract you from your own growth process. Then they *really* have power. Yours. As I told my daughter once after an odd lot of words were used in her school and town spelling bee (easy words toward the end, hard words at first, not evenly distributed): The best don't always win, and those who win aren't always the best. If you get mired down in jealousy and resentment and sport a pouty face, the only one really losing is you, by your own hand. Knock that off, *please.*

~ Hurdle #2: The Problem Might Be You ~

The problem is you. Well, it feels lousy to hear *that.* I'm being bold here, partly because I don't know you from Adam. I've known thousands of people like you, though, I'm sure. You're convinced that the world would be a better place if "they" knocked their crap off. "They" are always messing things up for you. "They" are incompetent, undermining, bullying, hopeless, disorganized, irresponsible, and downright stupid. "They" are ruining *everything.*

When I was interning at the addiction treatment facility back in graduate school, I was learning all about dysfunction and crazy. One day after a meeting with an addict and his family, I met with my supervisor to discuss the case. I started talking about "them" and "their problems" and how crazy "they" were. My supervisor, William, stopped me dead in my tracks and said, "change 'them' to 'me' and begin again." Wait…what?! I was talking about a crazy, addicted, dysfunctional family I was treating, not *myself.* This was not William's first time getting push back from an intern so he waited for me to catch up to his line of thinking. We ended up having a discussion about how whatever was true about "them" was also true about me, at least to some extent. Maybe the behaviors were different, but the human condition and experiences are pretty similar (fear, failure, control, needs, love, hate, disagreements). From that point forward, I was expected to start off each of our debriefs using "I" and "me" and "we."

See where I'm going with this yet? I consult with companies across the country and around the world as they try to set and reach their goals and undergo change management programs. There are a few companies I've had the pleasure of seeing from every angle, talking at an in-depth level to most, if not every one, of their functional departments. Do you know what they say when I ask them about the source of their problems? Every one of them lists another department. Not one of them says, "Oh, that's us. We are the source of the problem." It's always some other department(s). When you only talk to one department (especially if you're *in* the department), you might think that if I went to that other department – you know, the problem department – and waved my magic consultant wand that I could fix it all in a jiffy. Sorry, nope. No can do. Do you know why? Because it's very, very rarely one department's problem to fix. The truth is that every department has a role in the problem. Yes, I said it: Every department, even yours.

Until you take stock of how you are contributing to the problems you face, whether they be at work or at home, they aren't going to get much better. Start asking yourself what you might be doing to make the problem(s) worse or what you could be doing to make the problem(s) better. It's true what they say: Once you stop being part of the problem you can become part of the solution.

~ Hurdle #3: Putting Your Big Boy/Girl Pants On ~

Some of us forget to "act our parts," especially when stress sets in. We adults can do some pretty whacky things when we find ourselves in stressful situations, even if they are of our own doing. Most commonly, we regress. We stomp our feet like toddlers, raise our voices, get sarcastic and biting, teary-eyed, selfish, and we might even find ourselves on the couch curled up in fetal position sucking our thumbs and clinging to our blankie. And that's not cool. And, unless we have co-dependent family members or friends, it's not going to get us along the way to alleviating the stress. In fact, it's most likely going to compound it.

Unfortunately, just because someone has the title of "boss" or "mother" or some other "leadership" position doesn't mean that they are exempt from this debilitating behavior. So often I've witnessed people in power positions ignore their formal role when the going gets tough and becoming the equivalent of a 7-year old child who's had her favorite toy taken from her.

Getting personal, if you're a parent and something happens in your family (death of a close relative, divorce, etc.), you are obligated to put your big boy pants on and figure out a way to still be the parent. It's not okay to look to your children to feed your needs. Now, it's perfectly permissible to want to feel love and respect from your kids, to have a solid relationship based on trust, adoration, and (insert healthy feeling here). What's not okay is to "parentify" your children, to treat them like they are adults and on the same level playing field with you. They are not. Of course they're not, right? Yeah, only so often I see parents getting stompy and reactive when their kids misbehave and are hurtful toward their parents. I was asked by a mental health professional once, "do your kids ever tell you that they hate you." Ummm, yeah! If I let that make me crazy or resentful or pouty and I retaliate against them by withholding affection then who is the real child?

When I was a kid I was told that I was an "old soul" which became synonymous with "3 going on 30." Yes, I said three. One of the earliest stories of my uncanny ability to bring my mother comfort by being another "adult" came from when I was three. She imagined (hallucinated?) that I actually WAS an adult and that I came to her and gave her words of inspiration, which were enough to carry her out of the dark place she found herself in. My parents looked to me to be their sage and their solace, wanting me to provide sufficient reasons for them not to dive into their drugs habits or end their lives due to their oppressive depression.

I wish I was kidding, but, sadly, I'm not. And when I failed, when they used drugs or fell into paralyzing sorrow and isolation, I searched for reasons inside of ME for that failure. See, I hadn't read (or yet written!) *Feed The Need* so I was clueless about boundaries and all the psychological mumbo jumbo that would have alleviated some of the displaced responsibility I was holding. Looking back, it's so clear that it was wrong on every level to do this to a child: to seek to feed your needs through a child.

Now that I'm a mom, I'm exceptionally conscious about this dynamic. I'm not saying I'm perfect, mind you, but I am hyper vigilant about relying on my friends for advice, support, counsel, direction, and comfort…not my children. I'm notorious for saying the following to my kids when they ask about adult things that a bothering me, grilling me for details: "I have broad shoulders and good friends. I love you and I don't want you to concern yourself with my 'stuff.' I can handle what comes my way. You focus on being a kid, and a friend to your friends. I'll be the adult and do the same. Deal?"

Can you imagine saying that to your kids? If not, are you able to send that same message without saying those exact words? If you can't, it's time to take stock and own up to your behavior. Make a friend. Or two. Or seven. Find a support group. Start a journal. Just take a few steps back from your kids. They need to learn by living their own lives and holding themselves up as they grow, not being your emotional crutches. Parent them. Parent them by taking care of yourself first so you have the bandwidth to attend to their needs. You can't expect yourself to help anyone else on an empty tank.

That's the mistake most parents make in this arena: They confuse caring for their kids with martyring themselves for their kids. Martyrs makes for interesting literature but crappy parents. Martyrs, regardless of their feigned "strength" and "endurance" are needy as heck and end up sapping the very life force from those they are in relationship with. Including and especially their children. Kids are too often suckers for a needy and sad parent, jumping through every imaginable hoop to make things better. Kids haven't figured out how to set healthy boundaries in most cases, so they get sucked into a vortex that they have no easy exit from.

If you are reading about yourself in this section, fear not: It's not too late to change it. Every day you continue on this path, you do more damage to yourself and your kids. And, much like smoking, quitting the habit produces a multiplier of healing effects. Let your kids off the hook for meeting your needs and you will witness them taking ownership over their own and reaping those benefits.

It won't happen overnight. And your kids are likely to fight you on it. We get used to patterns of behavior, good and bad. Just because this shift is positive for them in the short- and long-run, it's change and they may resist it because they don't know what awaits them and they've gotten good and cozy in your dysfunctional universe. Help break them from that toxic orbit by turning off your gravitational pull (going to them to feed your needs) and flip a magnet instead (turn them away when they try to help, assuring them that "you got this").

What are *your* hurdles? What is it that holds you back from engaging fully in the change process? This step, Awareness, requires that you confront the ghosts and murmurs in the dimly lit areas of your brain so you can sweep the cobwebs out and address the issues that need addressing.

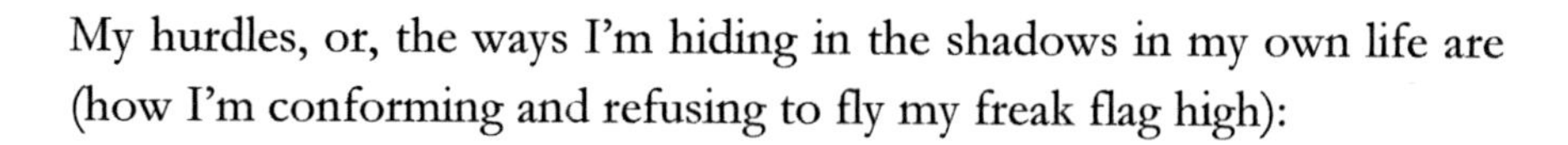

My hurdles, or, the ways I'm hiding in the shadows in my own life are (how I'm conforming and refusing to fly my freak flag high):

I'm afraid if I reveal these things about myself, the following will happen:

I've benefitted in the following ways from staying cloaked (e.g., pretending to be confident and competent when I'm not, I've attracted fans and associates who have benefitted my career).

"Nothing has a stronger influence psychologically on their environment, and especially on their children, than the unlived life of the parents." ~ C.G. Jung

~ Concluding Thoughts ~

Deepening and clarifying our awareness of what we seek to change is a necessary step in the change process. You may feel aware of being stuck, or maybe you just feel pain. Perhaps there isn't pain, necessarily, but you're not feeling the joy you want to feel. There's no rocket science in practicing Awareness, but presence and focus are required to take full advantage of this step. I've pointed out a few patterns that may be causing some of the problems in your life or company and how Awareness is the first step in getting you unstuck. Being aware of a problem is not good enough, however. You need to keep moving through the change process or you'll just have a whole lot of information about something that isn't going to be any different in a year than it is today. Unless, of course that "different" is "worse," because that could totally happen. Ready for the second step?

Key Chapter Concepts

- If you don't know something is broken, you can't fix it.
- Awareness is a muscle that can be toned by going to B-A-T (Be present, Ask questions, Try something new).
- Denial (and it's sister, Pretending) keep you stuck.
- Becoming aware of your hurdles to change allows you to get a game plan together to overcome them.

"Looking behind I am filled with gratitude.
Looking forward I am filled with vision.
Looking upwards I am filled with strength.
Looking within I discover peace." ~ *Q'ero* Indians

ACCEPTANCE

"The curious paradox is that when I accept myself just as I am, then I can change." Carl Rogers

~ Introduction ~

Congratulations! You've reached the step in the change process that is like the Holy Grail of guidance. It is the most commonly overlooked, and often actively avoided, step. Why? We've reviewed that we human beings have a strong need for control, traceable right down to our DNA for the purposes of survival. Being in control makes us *feel* safe often because it's what *keeps* us safe. Conversely, not being in control makes us anxious and uncomfortable. We want to feel safe so we try to exert control over everything we can.

This step – Acceptance – flies in the face of control. It means handing over control over the outcome which can feel mighty uncomfortable for many of us. If you're results-oriented it may seem like a foreign and downright insane concept to let go, especially when you're coming to the table with something you want to change. Isn't change an *active* process? Isn't it something that you *do*? Something that you take *charge* of? Are you freaking out yet? Take a deep breath (five if you're a self-proclaimed control freak). It's about to get **real**.

~ Elements of Acceptance ~

"If your compassion does not include yourself,
it is incomplete." ~ Buddha

In the spirit of simplicity, let's break Acceptance down into its simplest elements. There are two parts to acceptance:

1. *Looking in and back:* Accepting yourself the way you are, how you got here. Accepting that your present state is a direct result of your past decisions and actions. Accepting the past and present.
2. *Looking forward:* Accepting that you have to change, that things are going to change, and that you have work to do. Accepting the future.

This chapter is broken into these two main segments: *Acceptance of the past and present* and *acceptance of the future.* Additionally, I will address some hot topics that come up in the process of acceptance. The first thing we need to discuss, since both segments of the chapter rely upon it, is surrender. Deep breath. Aaaaahhhhhhh. You got this.

~ Surrender ~

Over the years I've worked with a lot of addicts. My second internship in my master's program in marriage and family therapy at UConn years ago was at an addiction recovery center so I came into relationship with countless addicts (the staff included!). To further prove my experience in this area, I grew up in a family of addicts. The difference between the ones I served and the ones I was raised by is that the ones I served were at least *on the surface* in a recovery process.

They were attending 12-Step™ meetings and therapy trying to slay their demons. If you're unfamiliar with the 12-Step™ program, the very first step in the recovery from addiction is to admit that you are powerless over your addiction. Powerless. When I first heard this it shook me up because, having grown up with a family of addicts who were *not* in recovery, the idea of giving up control was a foreign concept. In addiction recovery, it's really a matter of let go or be dragged.

What in the world does addiction recovery have to do with the Acceptance step of the change process? I just love how you ask me questions I'm about to answer!

The thing that both pieces of Acceptance (*looking in and back* and *looking forward*) and addiction recovery have in common is probably the most difficult aspect of Acceptance: Surrender. Surrender means to accept our state of being, knowing that we are not in control, particularly not of the past. It happened. It is what it is. You cannot change it so resisting it is pointless, and exhausting. Surrender gives you back your energy, the energy you're losing by fighting what is out of your control.

Be mindful that surrendering has layers. The first time you try to surrender know that the next time you may reach a deeper level of surrender. People who are practiced in the art of surrender often say, "this last time, I surrendered a little deeper." When you are practicing surrender, go as slowly as you feel good doing. When you do surrender, then and only then do you have a chance at a healthy existence. When you surrender, you relinquish control over something. Or, so we are led to believe.

Think about it for a minute. If you are in a battle (which uses the most common application of the term) and you surrender, you are giving up control over any number of things. At the very same time, you're taking control over the outcome. You are walking with your eyes open into the next phase of your path. There is great power in surrender because you are making the conscious decision to do so. Being beaten is different. You can surrender in the midst of a "win," though that isn't very common, I admit. Yet, it's possible. This change process is a battle of sorts. It's a battle between status quo and a new reality. A battle between what was and what will be. A battle between the old and the new. In order to "win" this battle, you will be required to accept the past, present, and future with all of their frustrations, wrongs, fears, and uncertainties. Speaking of "time," it's high time we got started.

~ Acceptance Of The Past & Present ~

"It's better to be absolutely ridiculous
than absolutely boring." ~ Marilyn Monroe

I could make this complicated, but I won't. You must accept things the way that they are before you can begin to move them to where you wish them to be. For those of you unfamiliar with my "meet them where they are" concept, let me offer a quick review. When you disagree with someone you can try to overpower them with your opinion and convince them. That's the approach most of us are most comfortable with and what we see practiced most often.

There's another way. You can "meet them where they are" and begin by seeing their position. You can accept the disagreement, knowing the fight will take away your personal power and peace. When you begin with compassion and seek understanding for their position (no matter how different it is), you neutralize the battle.

Think about the last time you got into an argument with someone. Did they tell you that you were wrong? How did that make you feel? Defensive? Agitated? Were you likely to say, "oh, you're right.

Thank you for pointing out the error of my ways. Gosh, golly gee, you're so helpful!" Probably not, unless you were being quite sarcastic. In fact, the more someone tells us we are wrong the more likely we are to defend ourselves. We often stop listening to the other person at all, vying for our next shot at telling them why *we* are right.

What does this have to do with accepting your past and present? In order to change something about yourself you have to have a conversation with your subconscious. You have to convince yourself that change is necessary. You need to get your subconscious to accept this path of change or you're going to slam into it at every turn.

Example: I have a client who possesses so much knowledge and so many tools to change her life but she keeps circling back to her old, ineffective way of doing things. She starts the process, then abandons it. She is a disappointment to herself. She knows she is capable of more, yet doubts that very assertion.

When I dug into it I found that she blamed it on *reluctance.* A reluctance to commit to another way of life. She abhors her reluctance. Sees herself as a pessimist, non-committal, and ineffective. She berates herself on a regular basis, blaming much of her dissatisfaction and circling of the emotional drain on this "trait."

Have you ever found yourself stuck like this? Able to pinpoint what you think is to blame for your troubles but that's where you stop? Caught in a firestorm of self-recrimination? It can end. You can leave this in the past. How?

~ Play Date With Your Inner Critic ~

By addressing your inner critic effectively. You need to develop trust with your inner critic. You have proven it right before. It's just like anyone else you have a relationship with: If you say one thing ("I want such and such") and do another, you've shown it that it can't trust what you say. It trusts what you *do*. You have to rebuild trust. You can acknowledge where you want to be, but still appreciate where you are and how you got there. Don't bother disagreeing with your subconscious; validate it. It weakens its fight. Like a rubber band snapping you back, don't run from it or it's going to sting. You *walk* with it, reassuring it that you hear the doubts and how you are calming it. If you read my book, *Feed The Need,* you know that the fourth need – Validation – is core to our happiness and trusting relationships. In the case of your subconscious, instead of receiving it from the outside, you have to deliver it on the inside.

Are you curious how I helped my "reluctant" client? Well, she had the tools but didn't use them long enough to make a difference and produce a shift in her behavior. So, I had her change her internal script from "I'm stuck and reluctant to change" to "I sometimes do things reluctantly." We discussed at length how being reluctant had served her in the past. She had to embrace the very thing she wanted to change. My advice to you: Love the thing that you hate about yourself. Hate creates dramatic tension. Love is warmth, freedom, calm, and acceptance. Love allows a trait to move freely; to dissipate. Love allows you to choose differently because you can recognize that your behavior is a choice and not a fatal flaw.

If you focus on what you don't want from yourself, you will reap more of it. If you say, "no more ice cream," what did you hear? I'll bet the two words that stuck with you weren't "no more," they were "ice cream." When you say "I want to lose weight," your body hears you insulting it, calling it "fat." If you do want to lose weight, you are probably apt to tell yourself flat out that you *are* fat. Your subconscious really wants you to be right. It seeks to build what you design. If you're designing a fat suit, your body will fill it out. Knock that crap off, would you please? This is the Acceptance step. Accept. You're carrying some "extra" weight. Alrighty then. Beating yourself up about it hasn't proven successful so are you ready to try something new? The missing link: Acceptance.

Accepting who you are and where you are. Yes, you. Acceptance, blah blah blah. Don't tell me to quit taking hits off the peace pipe. I mean this. You can either stay stuck, in a prison of your own design, or accept yourself exactly how you are, precisely where you are. It's a necessity. Your subconscious, child-like self that is underneath all of those layers of self-deception, criticism, and failure is constantly in battle mode, ready to prove to you that you are your own worst enemy and are doomed to be stuck exactly where you are. It's safer there and if you've done sufficient damage to your inner self by self-recrimination, your inner self is pretty angry with you. How can you make peace?

Offer praise for how it helped and protected you. Using the "fat" example, when you're fat AND unhappy about being fat it's a double whammy. If you accept yourself as fat, you might then be okay with being fat. You might be okay knowing that you are fat, and that it serves you in some ways. Maybe it's kept you safe from close relationships that seemed scary. Maybe it's kept you loyal to someone who told you that you were fat at some point along the way. If you accept that you're fat and you continue to want to change that about yourself, then you may proceed after this to the chapter on Analysis. You might read Analysis and then decide that you're okay where you are and you can put down the book before you read about Action.

We are not meant to be perfect. We are meant to be the best version of ourselves. Beauty would not exist if we were cookie cutter images of one another. We are supposed to be different. Being different isn't bad. Being perpetually unhappy and withdrawn from a full life IS bad. At least in my book.

How's that serving you? Really, seriously. How's that working for you? What's your payoff? That's a critical step to Acceptance. You must recognize what you are receiving from this negative behavior in order to accept its presence in your life.

Acceptance might be the hardest step. Some people think it's action, but this step is tougher. So much tougher. When you are on the Action step you're exerting control over your circumstances. You're in the driver's seat. You are moving toward something. You might even be racing toward it. You are large and in charge. Practicing acceptance is very different. It is the pause button, not the play button. It is quiet. It is reflection. It begins on the inside and is often not apparent on the outside. Except to the observant individual. When you are practicing Acceptance, just like when you are exhibiting anxiety and anger (by products of exerting control), you give off energy that is signaled to others. It communicates your state of mind and manner of being. And it evokes in-kind responses. If you *want* more calm, you must *be* more calm. If you want more crazy, have at it. You know what to do.

What's so tough about Acceptance? Oh, where should I start? First, it's not an active step which feels weird and uncomfortable to most of us. We are so used to a life of "doing" that we've forgotten (if we ever knew in the first place) how to " just be." We feel awkward just sitting and reflecting. Isn't there an e-mail we haven't responded to? A text we need to write? A report we need to review? A form we need to complete? A project we need to start? An article we need to read? There must be something to take us away from our thoughts and feelings?! Addiction often takes hold in this space, occupying that irksome feeling train track.

Acceptance is also the forgotten step because it's not intuitive. We are taught to think that we need to **hate** where we are in order to rail against it and move on to where we need to be. We talk about being *sick* of a certain experience in order to change it. Hate spurs us to move. We don't want to bathe in sludge and smelly nastiness, so we implore ourselves to move away from it. We aren't inclined to *accept* it;

we are moved to resent it. We believe that if we hate it enough it will guarantee that we never return to it. Take smoking, for example. We call smokers "butt heads" and "ashtray lickers" (well, at least that's what I call them...) and concoct commercials that show the disgusting effects of the habit.

Does this get people to quit smoking? Not really. What it does accomplish is getting non-smokers to think even worse things about smokers and smokers to think even worse things about themselves. *When we feel badly about ourselves we are far less likely to hold the energy and commitment necessary to grab hold of a change process and complete it.* Instead, we want to hide under the covers and wish the situation away. It's why you tend to see trim and fit people at the gym more than the tragically out of shape, and this phenomenon gives rise to home gyms and fitness contraptions and videos you can use in the comfort of your own home. How many people do you see posting their "before" photos until they can post an "after" right alongside it. We reject our current selves in order to pave the path to our desired selves. This, folks, is a recipe for failure.

Accepting yourself as you are, exactly how you are and where you are, is the missing link. Acceptance. Refusing to fight, blame, and malign yourself. Denying your natural tendency to self-flagellate and beat the holy heck out of yourself. Turning down the volume of the critical voices in your head that tell you what a failure you are or how terrible you are for doing whatever it is that you do in the way you do it. Acceptance requires that you see yourself as you are right now, today, and focus on that, not on where you desire to be at some future day and time.

How is your relationship with your inner critic? Does he/she drag you down, giving you excuse after excuse for your lackluster existence?

Do you readily agree with your inner critic or do you attempt to smother him/her, denying that he/she has a point?

"I will not let anyone walk through my mind
with their dirty feet." ~ Gandhi

~ Whom Can You Trust? ~

All of that "agreeing with your inner critic" sounds completely crazy, right? It flies in the face of everything we've been taught! You're supposed to "keep your eyes on the prize" and "keep the end in sight." Yeah, well, those are catchy anecdotes but they miss a critical, and almost always overlooked, step in the change process. Acceptance isn't just a new-age, positive-thinking popular fad; it's at the core of why your change efforts have crashed and burned in the past. Why? Lack of trust. What? What does a lack of trust have to do with change? So much! It's all rooted in that pesky little player called your subconscious.

Over time, we've all amassed a certain number of failures. We've wanted things for our lives that we haven't succeeded in attaining. Maybe we've tried and failed. Maybe our failure is in our lack of trying at all, avoiding failure altogether (or so we think). Perhaps it's that stubborn 5-10 (or 50) pounds of extra weight that we just can't seem to shake off. Or, it's our resolution to be on time to appointments. It could be our vow to stay on top of our finances and stay out of debt.

Whatever our failures may be, our subconscious has been keeping score. By "keeping score" I mean to the level of your favorite uncle who can recount the stats from every player on their favorite team (or the entire league) for the past 40 years. Our subconscious knows every stumble, every broken promise, and every negative thing we've said to ourselves along the way. We've said over and over that we've got to change, yet we don't. So what has our subconscious heard?

- You hate this aspect of yourself.
- You need to change, but..
- You don't change.
- You expect this aspect of yourself to continue.
- You talk a good game but you won't really change.

What negative messages has your subconscious been hearing all these years? What have you been telling yourself about *you*? What messages have you been hearing from other people that you haven't shut down? What changes have you been telling yourself that you must make happen? Take a few minutes and write them down here.

Now is as good a time as any to meet your monster.

~ Monster Under Your Bed ~

"If you hear a voice within you saying, "You are not a painter,"
then by all means paint…and that voice
will be silenced." ~ Vincent van Gogh

I know, I know, you're not six years old anymore. Of course you don't believe in monsters under your bed. Guess what? I don't believe you. I haven't yet met a person who doesn't have a monster (or an entire village of them) under their beds. Think I've lost my mind? Nope. You have at least one monster, one fear that keeps you from doing something. The biggest problems with having a monster under your queen-sized bed is that you don't even know what it looks like. Does it have two horns or none? One eye or three? Is it furry or does it have scales? My recommendation: Make friends with it. Look at it. Monsters are much less scary in the light.

What does "bringing your monster into the light" mean, practically speaking? It means that you need to fully examine your fear. Since this is the Acceptance step, your job here is to accept that you *have* a monster. You must accept that you have a fear monster holding you back from going after your dreams and realizing your potential.

One of my clients a few years back was treading water in his career. If anyone was stuck, it was this guy. When I probed to find out what was holding him back from taking the necessary steps to grow his business, he responded that he might fail and he didn't want to risk that. So, he circled the drain and consistently felt like he was falling short. Want to know what I told him? I told him, "you might be right. You might fail and lose it all." He was so appreciative! I'm kidding. Instead he said, "you're a terrible coach!" I chuckled because I knew where I was going with this. Curious?

It's pretty simple. If you try to man handle or wrestle down your demons, they usually win. They have a great deal of power. They've been in charge of you for years (decades, even). Think they'll just step aside because you read some inspiring coffee table book filled with "success" quotes? Please. They want to hold their position, in part because they want to keep you safe. Instead of arguing with your monsters, acknowledge them. They have a point, don't they? You've proven them right repeatedly…right? Stop telling them they're wrong or they'll keep showing up to demonstrate that they are right. That you're a failure. That the world is a scary place. That risk is scary.

They're not wrong. Not completely, anyway, so acknowledge the voice. Agree with its experience then ask it permission to show it another way, to offer another possible outcome. Direct your attention to the monsters instead of denying their existence. When you introduce yourself to the monster hiding under your bed it becomes less scary. The fear of the unknown is demolished. And, *you* just claimed more of your personal power.

~ Acceptance of the Future ~

"Eighty-seven percent of people allow their fear of failure to outweigh their desire to succeed." ~ Les Brown.

Part of accepting the future is letting go of the past. In order to develop new ways of being, you must grieve the loss of the person you were, the life you knew, and the pain you caused yourself (and others). Before you can release the past and welcome in the new, you have to grieve the old. There was comfort and safety in the old ways of doing things. There were upsides to it, for sure, or you wouldn't have gone on as long as you did. Sadly, there was a lot of pain and discomfort, too. The longer you've been stuck, the more pain you've logged. You may have exerted a heap of effort fighting your patterns and you just got more stuck. As hard as that path has been, you've grown to know it, like an old pair of slippers. Leaving it behind might be worse, you tell yourself.

Change *is* scary. In order to get the life you want, you have to accept the fear and uncertainty. What if you fail? What if you change yourself and nothing around you changes? What if you lose relationships you once held dear? What if you're on this change path and you end up less happy/successful than you are now and conclude that you should have just stayed put?

You can literally "what if" yourself to death if you're not careful. Remember your control buckets? Most of these "what ifs" are not in your locus of control. You can control how you think, feel, and behave – and react – to any of these scenarios. You can influence the daylights out of some of these things, strategically and intentionally using your thoughts, feelings, and actions. What other people do, and what the eventual outcomes of your changes are, is not in your control.

Do you want life to get better? Focus on **you**. Glance at others; attend to their needs and tendencies so that you can use your influence well. But, put your full focus on **you**. That's where your power is. Using your power to make you the best person you can be is the only moral and effective use of power. It's not the power that is dominion over others, but empowerment of yourself to take up your space in your chair.

~ Space In Your Chair ~

Some time ago, I was meeting with a client and he was talking about a book he was writing. It was a truly riveting novel, set in his home culture, something I knew little about. In setting the framework for the book and his purpose to enlighten others, my client mentioned an expert on the topics he was tackling. This expert was someone he deeply revered and their ideas meshed and supported one another's. He described how his work would be building on the work of his hero.

Being my outspoken self, I asked him if he was asking this person if he would write the foreword to his book? My client responded with embarrassment and surprise, saying the polite equivalent of, "hell, NO!" I got pretty bossy at this point and in a very passionate way I demanded to know when he was planning to take up the space in his own chair? As I saw it, he was sitting tentatively on the edge of his chair – his current place in the world – not owning his power, influence, and potential contributions. What a waste. No one else will take up the space in *his* chair. And, that goes for you, too.

You're the only one who can fill up your chair. If you're not doing all that you can do to grab ahold of your power you're just wasting the space given to you. You need to open up to the power that you possess by knowing who you really are and what you are all about. Instead of asking the questions "why?" or "how?" you must start asking "why not?" and "how could I not?"

I believe that it's about inhibitions. Inhibitions keep our behavior within certain limits. They tell us when to calm down, speak softer, walk more gently, and live more quietly. They instill fear in us; fear that leads us to conform to group norms and the expectations of others. They keep us safe. Safe from reprisal and rejection. Being uninhibited is freeing but can be scary as hell. Being uninhibited makes us vulnerable to the judgments of others.

What will people think if I do such and such? Will they reject me? Think less of me? How can I make them understand why I want to do this and that? What if they think I'm silly or careless or, worse, not capable? Knowing that you're dying reduces the power of that fear of reprisal. It's not that it wouldn't exist; it's just that you wouldn't be around long enough for any of its effects to hit you. We tend to live constrained lives because we fear the long-term effects of the judgments of others. We want to feel accepted and supported and if we do anything "crazy" we might get kicked to the curb. Newsflash, people: You *are* dying. A little more every day.

Remember art class as a kid? Even in this "creative" space, did you get rewarded for staying inside the lines and following the directions to a "t," or for creating your own expressive piece?

Creativity within a structure isn't necessarily creativity at all. Controlled creativity is a shell of creativity. What purpose does the social threat of reprisal serve?

Control. It's all about control. Controlling people's actions so that mayhem doesn't follow. Rules (social norms and conventions) keep people under control by keeping their behavior within expected, normal limits. Art projects would be so much harder to grade if the teacher just let students follow their inspiration. Life might be more difficult to "grade" if the standards were evaluated by individuals and not the group. Imagine that? Living in a world where you get to choose how you define "success?"

Pssst….we do. People live like that all around you. Well, maybe not around *you*. If your corner of the world is anything like mine, you're surrounded by people who are stuck in the rat race of pretense and masks and trying to outdo the Jones'. I call it "FaçadeVille."

You keep racing toward who knows where, only sure of one thing: Keeping up appearances is job number one. Not happy in your marriage? No one cares. Decorate the house, send out the holiday cards, post endearing photos of the not-so-happy couple on Facebook™, and show up to events together. Fight in private. Or, stop fighting altogether because you know it doesn't matter anymore. No fight is ever going to get resolved or make things better.

Hate your job? Keep quiet. It pays the bills for the lifestyle you've agreed to. Wake up with dread but don't let it show. Numb out. Stop feeling much of anything so you don't have to feel the disappointment in your choices. You've resigned yourself to the "life" you've created. And in so doing, you've shut down your potential.

Have you had enough?

~ Pipeline of Awesome ~

"The meaning of life is to find your gift,
the purpose of life is to give it away." ~ Joy J. Golliver

I certainly hope so! Which brings me to one of my most favorite concepts about human nature: ***The Pipeline of Awesome***, which is closely related to my "Space In Your Chair" analogy. The biggest difference is that the Pipeline of Awesome refers to your divine purpose whereas the Space In Your Chair could be any old chair you're sitting in. Making a change in the direction of your true purpose commands that you open your Pipeline of Awesome. Accepting that path is exciting, to say the least! Your Pipeline is powerful and demands that you open it up and share it with the world. When you resist that inclination to hold it back and you stop keeping your awesomeness to yourself, it means that you are *open*. When you are open to it, you taste the sweetness of surrender. In case you've been hating on surrender, it's another way that surrender serves you.

There's little room for conformity if you're invested in opening up your Pipeline of Awesome, full throttle. In order to accept the parameters of the Pipeline of Awesome, you're going to have to accept rejection. And judgment. And maybe even some straight-on hate. I mean it. *Hate*. People who are living lives of façade and limitations don't often take too kindly to people who don't. You're rejecting the status quo which forces two truths to the surface:

1. There is *choice* in accepting or rejecting it.
2. There might be something on the other side that makes rejecting it worth it.

With choice comes responsibility and a whole legion of people have come to believe that they are victims of their circumstances. It's just not true. You always have choices. Always. The choices might be ugly but they exist. When you start seeing the choices you can own yours; take responsibility for what you've chosen.

How are you living smaller than you could? Are you apologizing for being more than others are comfortable with you being? I used to sit on the side of my chair, too. I did. I had a job, a marriage, two amazing kids, and some terrific friends. What I didn't have was myself. I was living inside a small space, on the edge of my chair, not being myself in any real way. I loved people, I did activities, but I wasn't joyful, passionate, or expansive. I was *existing*, but I wasn't living up to my potential or giving the sum of my gifts to anyone. I wasn't comfortable in my own skin and it showed.

Fast forward ten years: I was talking with a budding entrepreneur and he was hesitating in getting his product to market. All the signs were there that his product was going to be well-received because everyone (every last person, I swear) who had seen what he was making was "ooh"ing and "aah"ing non-stop. His hesitation was ticking me off something fierce because my worldview was triggered by his hesitance. "How?" you ask? Simple.

I believe that we are put on this earth to use our love, our gifts, our vision, and our passions to make the world fuller for having had us. When we don't use what was given to us for the advantage of the world, we are thumbing our noses to the very entity that created us. We are being wasteful. When we let low self-esteem, lack of confidence, procrastination, and any practice like it get in the way of us sharing our gifts with the world, we are robbing the planet of our abundance. My family is from California and it seems that almost every year they are threatened by devastating wildfires due to drought conditions. Hillsides are engulfed in flames and residents are evacuated, running for their lives. People lose their houses, belongings, and sometimes their lives to these tragic occurrences. The answer to preventing these fires? Ummm, rain. Just rain. Okay, and no one throwing cigarette butts near bushes. But you get my drift. If they had more rain, they'd have fewer fires.

So what does this have to do with the "Pipeline of Awesome." I really do love it when you ask me these questions so I can make my point. Imagine a pipeline, one that carries water in immense volumes, coming straight from the source of all water (the heavens). Now imagine that this "water" is your essence, your true and intended self, your unique combination of gifts and talents and experiences, and that the "heavens" represents whatever entity you associate with your higher power. There is so much destruction in this world, like those California wildfires. When we open our Pipeline of Awesome we can dampen that destruction and create new life.

Someone asked me at a conference the other day what my "why" is. Why do I spend my time, energy, and passion on my chosen career? It's to open the Pipeline of Awesome for everyone who is willing to do so. Can you imagine opening the floodgates to your own potential? Actually living your truth? Doing what you were meant to do and doing it with vigor and unapologetic enthusiasm? Charging your clients what you are worth and not some number that doesn't scare you to ask for? The world will be richer for YOU putting YOU into the world. Can I tell you something? Of course I can because I'm writing this book so I get to say any darn thing I want. Anyway.... It's not just a *shame* if you don't open up your Pipeline of Awesome: It's criminal. That's right. I said it. You're committing a crime against your very humanity if you don't open that baby up. Not just letting some of it trickle out. You are *required* to share your gifts and your passion with other people. It's in the contract you signed before you landed your sweet self on this planet. You don't remember?

Too bad. What's that they say? "Ignorance of the law is no excuse." This world was not created for "average" and "boring." Ever look at the Grand Canyon? Niagara Falls? Machu Picchu? How about a butterfly's wings? The petals of a flower? These things are downright magnificent. And so are you. Maybe you're not feeling so magnificent today, and that's okay. You're going to use the tools in this book to claim your Pipeline of Awesome. Get ready to say "goodbye" to living a life that is less than the one you're capable of claiming. The Pipeline of Awesome isn't necessarily about wealth or fame or climbing the corporate ladder. It is about living with the appreciation that there are no do-overs.

This is not a dress rehearsal. It's the real deal. If you're banking on living until you're 100 years old, that's fantastic. Even if you do (which, statistically speaking is highly unlikely), how many years do you have left? How would you like to leave your mark on the world? No, you don't have to invent the equivalent of Google™ to make that happen. In my not-so-humble opinion, when you reach the end of your life, you're not going to be judged on the car you drive, house you live in, career path you've mastered, or the savings account you've squirreled away. Nope. I think you'll be asked a few questions: "Did you love everyone the best you could? Did you leave everything better than you found it? Did you have fun with all the great stuff down there? *Did you use the gifts I gave you and share them with the world?*" If you focus your energies on opening up your Pipeline of Awesome you'll pass that test with flying colors. Want to know a secret? Even if I'm wrong, the 100 years you have on this planet are going to be much more amazing. Think you oughta give it a shot?

Let's get practical about this. What if Taylor Swift had decided that she should be an accountant instead of an award-winning vocalist? If accounting was her passion and she felt alive when she was doing balance sheets then by all means it would have been the best decision – for her and for the world. So, it's not about fame and fortune. It's about living the life you are capable of living, using the gifts that you have. Living your potential. Not making excuses for why it's hard: Stepping up and making it happen. If you were given a death sentence, what would you do with your last breaths? What part of yourself would you want to share with the world, even your little corner of it? Before you make some argument about Taylor Swift being somehow different than you, maybe she is because of her raw talent, but she was bullied as a kid so she had reasons to shut down and walk away from any undue attention and to feel badly about herself. What did she do instead? She used her pain to make her famous by writing about the people and experiences that hurt her.

I still get tears in my eyes every time I hear Tim McGraw's "Live Like You Were Dying" because the premise of the song is a heartfelt recommendation to live each day like it's your last, taking chances and being the best you can be in every moment. Imagine the power of that? Of harnessing all of your energy to act upon the world instead of having it act upon you? That's the Pipeline of Awesome at work. Why does facing that your time is expiring quickly change your behavior? It's about surrendering to your finiteness. We are nothing if not finite. Like we discussed, you might find yourself all alone if you open up your pipeline. Now I'll ask you: Ready to open that pipeline up? It's time to interview yourself.

What is the gift that you have to share with the world? If you can't readily list one, ask yourself what your friends and colleagues tend to say about you and what they can count on you to do.

How open is your pipeline? Are you holding off in letting it flow until "someday" or are you investing time and energy into letting it flow now?

If you don't know if it's clogged or not, you can't open it up full-force. Spend some time now figuring out where you are so you can get to where you want to be, before someday rolls around.

~ Lonely Only One ~

I have coached countless executives, team members, and done personal coaching with individuals who stayed stuck for one compelling reason: What if they are the only one who changes? What if no one else tries and they put in all sorts of effort all by themselves? Most of us have been burned at one time or another, even if it was being chosen last on the playground, by trusting others to stick with us and being left all alone to face something we thought we'd have company for.

Guess what? You may be right. You may be the only one changing. Or, you may be the only one actively, purposefully changing. As my mom used to drill into my skull, the person with more awareness in the relationship (or situation) is the one with more responsibility. "More responsibility" includes the responsibility to make changes to improve the situation or relationship, even if the other person isn't doing anything. Because, at the end of the day, you're the one who has to wake up with yourself every day. *They* aren't accountable to you. *You* are accountable to you.

It's a hard pill to swallow, I know. My mother taught me this and it was a real pain in my kiester. She explained that because I was the one with more awareness and emotional capability I was also the one who had to take the higher road, be the more responsible one in the relationship with my sister. But I'm the baby sister!? That's not fair! Fair, schmair. Tough noogies. I admit that I didn't always follow all of my mother's advice but this piece I did, more often than not.

Like she was reaching back from the grave, my mom was whispering this in my ear shortly after she died when things got crazy with my sister. It was a very difficult time, but this advice got me through it, sanity intact. I witnessed my sister being erratic and destructive in her pain and I knew that my mom would be urging me to "let it go," knowing that I had the capacity to detach from crazy behavior and move forward. So I did. And so can you.

Want some good news? When you make positive changes, you get stronger. Even the other people who might abandon you in this change initiative are apt to be affected by your changes. I must prepare you, though. If they aren't reading this book, they may not be getting comfortable with the concept of change so they might be terrified of it. As a direct result, they may confront your efforts at change with an equal and opposing force.

That's okay, though, because you read this page and you'll see it coming from a mile away. You'll be prepared. You won't react. You'll know they are doing what they are doing out of habit, fear, and self-preservation. You won't judge them for that. You'll email me if you need to, kind of like calling your sponsor. I'll talk you down off the ledge. If you keep at the changes you're making, chances are that others will start to follow suit and the system (that blasted organization you're part of) will start to shift. If you get frustrated waiting for that or the change goes off the rails, please email me and we will orchestrate an intervention. It's not my first time...

~ Feel The Suck ~

Pretty catchy, eh? I'm notorious for facing even the most frightening and frustrating situations with some aspect of cheer. Actually, the worse the situation, the more my pearly whites shine. I can figure just about anything out, given a few minutes to regroup. Having been raised by two depressed (often suicidal) parents, I had the "job" of pulling them out of their despair; being their reason for living. So, when I face my own trials and tribulations, I'm quick to make some chipper remark, reframe the bad situation into a "growth opportunity" or some such thing. Off I skip to tackle it, push through it, or overcome it, forever hopeful.

A few years back, I had hit a massive wall of trouble. It was bad. It followed a whole trail of other bad stuff that had plagued me for years and I was tired. No, I was freaking exhausted. I needed a break and I couldn't seem to catch one. I called my friend, Lisa, and gave her my update. Being my usual self, I put lipstick on that pig and was making the best of it. She stopped me dead in my tracks. She told me to knock it off. When Lisa tells me to do something, I listen. Well, most of the time and usually sooner rather than later. In that conversation we coined the term, "feel the suck."

We agreed that my current situation was terrible. It downright sucked. If I breezed past that truth I wasn't being fair or honest. She gave me permission to feel badly about my circumstances, to embrace the "suck" instead of trying to deny it. It was painful but real. I was finally being honest with myself and I took the first step toward trusting myself. When I was busy ignoring the hurt I was feeling, I was also busy telling myself that it wasn't okay to feel it, even though it was perfectly okay.

That's a recipe for disaster. I had been confused for many years about what "strength" meant and Lisa set me straight that day. Being strong wasn't simply about overcoming the obstacles put in front of me. Acknowledging that sometimes life hands you some pretty hefty burdens and feeling that pain takes strength.

Want to show off your big, burly muscles? Cry. Scream. Pout. Be real for a minute when you're tempted to glaze right over the crap at your doorstep. It stinks and no amount of air freshener can make that untrue. Accept that life (and people) suck sometimes. Feel the suck. Then, and only then, move forward.

~ Slip and Slide ~

In your journey toward change, you may find yourself skipping along, making positive strides and really jazzed about it. Then you'll slip. Then you'll slide. You might be reading this book because that's exactly what happened to you and you've been stuck where you slipped back to ever since. Part of accepting your past, present, and future is accepting that you will, indeed, slip and slide sometimes. It doesn't mean that you're a poser, big faker, or lying to yourself that you can make a change. It's simply part of the process. Accept that. Be okay with the slip, knowing that it's giving you an opportunity to see something about yourself, others, and the world around you. Use that information in the next step – Assessment – to move you forward again.

~ Concluding Thoughts ~

The most common complaint I hear about change is that people are "trying so hard" to make something different in their lives and aren't seeing the results they are seeking. It's like they think that the harder they push, the more likely they are to succeed. We praise "fighters" in our society. We commend hard work. We respect blood, sweat, and tears in the pursuit of a goal. All these things are admirable, for certain. There is, however, a time and a place for them: *After* acceptance.

In boxing, there is tremendous energy lost in the fight. If you're trying so hard to throw punches, you'll quickly exhaust yourself. When we are going through life, the same rule applies: Fighting is exhausting. You picked up this book because you want (or are facing) a change and you want a solution. The Acceptance step is your "rest" step. You've most likely been trying *so* hard. Stop trying. Stop trying to force things. Taking time to grieve. Time to pout. In order to have Emotional Agility, we need to use the tools in this chapter to structure our minds to accept ourselves where we are.

Key Chapter Concepts

- Two parts to Acceptance: Accepting who/where you are and Accepting that change is coming.
- Surrender is hard, but necessary to true and lasting change
- Fighting your subconscious is an energy suck. Make friends with your inner critic and diminish its power.
- Be ready to take up the space in your chair and open your pipeline of awesome.
- Accept than you're bound to slip as you make changes.

"They tell us from the time we're young to hide the things
that we don't like about ourselves, inside ourselves.
I know I'm not the only one who spent so long
attempting to be someone else.
Well, I'm over it." ~ Mary Lambert

6

ASSESSMENT

"It takes as much energy to wish
as it does to plan." ~ Eleanor Roosevelt

~ Introduction ~

Have you ever gotten in your car to go on an errand and when you get to your destination you don't even remember the process of getting there? You went on autopilot which means that you weren't really present during the drive. Is that safe? Probably not so much. This step in the change process is usually approached with the same attentiveness. For those of you who have unknowingly followed the five-step process, I'll make a bet that most of you skipped right through the last step and this one, too, saying something like, "I know I need to change things because they are bad. They will get better and there will be endless rainbows and sunshine on the other side of my efforts." It's inviting, to forge ahead with wild abandon, but if you don't get this step right you won't have a map to get you to where you want to go and you'll stay stuck where you are indefinitely.

This book offers you the opportunity to change your life and your circumstances, to carve the future as you want it to be. In order to do that, you need to conduct an honest inventory of where you are so you can figure out where you want to be. Don't answer the questions and assessments how you think you *should*; answer truthfully, candidly. You're reading a book about change for crying out loud! There's no sense in kidding yourself on the Assessment step. Do you know what that will get you? A whole plate load of nothing. Just more of the same. You can't go for a swim in the ocean if you stay standing on the shore. Jump in. Get real or get going.

In this chapter, I will provide a series of questions to answer about where you are in your growth process. I've broken down the topic into easy-to-navigate segments, assessing your:

- Relationship contracts
- Lessons from the past
- Current state
- Control tendencies and risk tolerance
- Emotional agility
- Desired state

In addition, I will also give you a chance to assess the landscape, the contextual issues that may influence your change process, positively or negatively.

~ Mirror, Mirror On The Wall ~

When was the last time you looked at yourself in the mirror? Not just looking for clogged pores or to get your makeup on flawlessly. But really LOOKED. I worked with a man once who (really) looked in the mirror at himself one day, didn't like what he saw and literally said to himself, "I'm making a change TODAY." And he did. Why? Because he stopped and actually looked at himself, saw where and who he was and wasn't pleased with his current state. He focused. I liken it to when people say, "Did you hear me?" after they've shared something important and we say, "Of course. I was listening." If we were totally honest, though, we know we might have heard the words they were saying but we didn't give them our focus, our complete, undivided, purposeful attention. If we had, we would have connected more deeply to them and been able to give them a truer response.

The same thing goes for conversing with ourselves. If we take a moment, even every so often, to look into our own eyes, check in with ourselves, we can deepen our relationship with ourselves and expand our personal power. Focus makes productivity a reality and helps relationships to flourish. That's why "focus" is my favorite "f" word, ever! In order to get this step right and really assess ourselves and the change we are facing properly, we need to focus. Assessment demands clarity and honesty and focus. Don't we deserve to give that to ourselves?

Aside from assessing ourselves directly, we also need to assess our relationships and the expectations we hold about them.

~ Relationship Contracts ~

"Expectation is the root of all heartache." ~ William Shakespeare

Did you know that you have a relationship contract with everyone in your life? You don't remember signing it? You did. You agreed to a set of expectations that each of you could have about each other. Expectations that may or may not have been discussed, but that each of you hold about the other person. Maybe it's that they will always tell you the truth, no matter how hurtful. Maybe it's that you will always keep things light and cheerful, staying away from anything deep and meaningful. People sign these contracts every day when they enter into relationships and set up their "dance," their relationship dynamic. Figuring out what those contracts are is worth investigating. Why?

Ahh, so many reasons. First off, I'm a huge proponent of awareness. If you are aware of something, you can make deliberate actions versus just going along for the ride. Second, when you see your relationships as based on these contracts, you can see how certain agreements might not be serving you. You can appreciate that it's not necessarily about who the other person is or who you are; it's about the relationship contract you both signed. Lastly, when you can see your relationship contracts clearly, you can trust the people you're in relationship with to be exactly as the contract spells out. Well, that is, unless or until they decide to change the contract.

When I was in a serious relationship years ago, I performed this very assessment. I was in a verbally and emotionally abusive relationship and was feeling increasingly miserable. The man I was involved with hadn't changed during our relationship: He had been abusive from jump. I knew who he was when I started dating him, yet I continued to be with him. I signed a relationship contract that permitted him to hurt me and for me to feel responsible for his wrath. I went along with this contract for almost a decade.

At one pivotal point, I used my training as a marriage and family therapist to see our relationship through a lens of roles we were playing and rules we were abiding by. It was through this perspective that I could see our contract, and I decided that I wanted to amend it. Transform it, really. I didn't want to be "that girl" anymore. I was changing, opening up my own Pipeline of Awesome and this contract wasn't a fit for who I was becoming.

So, I told him I wanted to change our contract and we did and we lived happily ever after. Yeah, not so much. I did tell him I wanted to change our contract (and I put it in language like that). He didn't care. He was comfortable in our contract and saw no need to change it. He saw me as violating the contract because he didn't think that contracts could or should be changed. Ever. What good did it do for me to know about all this contract stuff if he wasn't going to change? It was central to me getting clear and staying as peaceful as I could as I let go of the relationship. I knew that I had signed the contract, too, so I had allowed his behavior. I was not responsible for his abusive treatment of me, mind you. But, I was able to accept his anger at me wanting to change the contract because he didn't sign on for that.

This is your cue to assess your relationship contracts, to see if they serve you and your plan for change. Here are some questions to ask yourself about your relationships (personal and professional) to see if your contracts might need to be updated or rewritten entirely.

- What are the rules about your relationship (who is allowed/supposed to do what?)?

- What have you agreed to that now feels uncomfortable or yucky?

- Are there déjà vu moments where you're aggravated again about something that went on between you?

See anything interesting? Think it might be time to renegotiate?

Before I saw relationship contracts, I had a huge issue with trust. Like you, I'd been hurt in the past and vowed to never let it happen it again. But it did, over and over again. I trusted less and less as time went on. I was left feeling anxious and resentful. When I was able to see the contracts in my relationships, the ways in which I agreed to be a certain way and tolerate a certain level of behavior from others, I began trusting people to be who they are, where they are. A magical thing happened that changed my life forever: My expectations about others started to equal reality. Expectations equaled reality. I wasn't falling from the tower of expectations onto the cold, hard ground of reality. They were one in the same.

This process is not about lowering your expectations; it's about *righting* them. You can trust absolutely everyone: To be who they are, in the situation they are in, conditions they are under, and within the contract they signed. Putting *our* hopes and expectations on others instead of simply observing them gets in the way of our happiness and initiates all kinds of stress.

Please don't get me wrong: I have screwed this up plenty of times since. I have this pesky little thing called "hope" that gets in the way of having expectations equal reality. I *hope* that people will be who I need them to be instead of who they are. I let my hope for my needs getting met (someday) to eclipse what they are likely to do. What's that saying? "Inspect before you expect." You can better align expectations with reality when you're informed.

Character is demonstrated by actions, not words. Watch what people do; what they spend their time and money on. It's very revealing. When someone tells you that you are important to them and that they value things about you that their other relationships don't offer, but then they opt to spend their time and resources on those other relationships, believe their actions. It might sound nicer in their head to say that they value the things they say they do, but the truth is revealed in their actions. Who you are is who you spend the most time with and invest the most energy in. Be careful. As Maya Angelou said, "People show you who they are. Believe them the first time."

Here's a visual to keep in mind the next time you're tempted to expect someone to be someone who you want them to be versus who they've shown themselves to be:

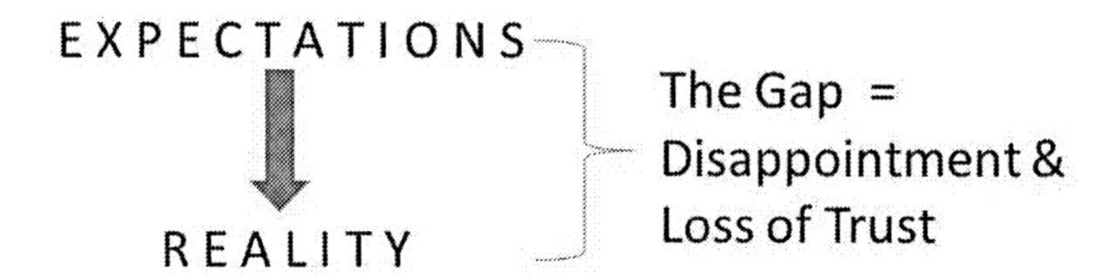

Property of Dr. Bridget Cooper, 2015

The fall from expectation to reality hurts. We call it "disappointment." How much does it hurt when someone calls you a "disappointment?" Or tells you that you've disappointed them? It's hard to hear. We've fallen from grace. How do we get ourselves tangled up in these disappointments over and over again? It goes back to trust and understanding. When I say "trust" I mean choosing how much you should trust. When I say "understanding" I don't mean blind compassion and being a doormat. Trusting people to be who they are, where they are.

If you trust your best friend to be chummy with you in the workplace when she's targeting a big promotion, you're going to feel let down. Did she not act like a friend? Perhaps not the friend she is to you outside of work, but that's not a bad thing. She's different in work because her priorities are different there based on her choices and desires: To be a professional success. She might jump in front of a moving train for you when you're socializing in the city on the weekend. But if she's professionally ambitious, make no mistake: She might be just this side of cordial at the office if she perceives that anything beyond that may be seen as unprofessional.

~ Assessing Lessons From The Past ~

Leaving the past in the past is a terrific adage but it doesn't do you any good if you haven't already learned from your past before you put it to rest. "Those who cannot remember the past are condemned to repeat it" (Santayana, 1905) is a much more helpful framework. In the Assessment phase, it's critical to take a brief look back at your life so you can recognize patterns that may or may not be serving you as you embark on a path of change.

Since I don't know you, I certainly cannot attest to your path to this point. I don't know if you've had a tough go of it, or if your life has been a cakewalk. I'd wager that even if by some accounts you've had it fairly easy, we all get bumped and bruised along the way. Right after my dad died when I was 24, I found a t-shirt that read "when life gives you scraps, make a quilt." I bought it on the spot and wore that with pride for many months. I really do try to live by the tenet that it's not what happens to you, but how you handle what happens to you, that matters. Are you ready to put that into play? To make the best of what's happened in your life? Then it's time to interview yourself so you can get a handle on how you're allowing your negative past experiences to affect you today.

What are the worst things that have ever happened in your life?

1.

2.

3.

What lessons about the world (and yourself) did you learn from these experiences?

1.

2.

3.

When have you had to revisit these lessons (when has history repeated itself)? Did you realize that you were in a déjà vu moment right away or did it take you some time to figure it out?

Do you feel stronger or weaker as a result? Explain.

I have an e-mail subscription to "Notes from the Universe™" (thanks, Mike Dooley!) which means that I get daily inspiration about my potential and the abundance of the Universe. One of the underlying principles of these notes is that we have control over our destinies through our thoughts and making deliberate actions toward the life we want for ourselves. The notes from the universe tell us that thoughts become things, so if we can master our thoughts we can master occurrences. If that's true then we are in control of our thoughts AND external events. I disagree. We influence them strongly, but we have to focus on our influence not on the outcome because the sheer chaos of the universe dictates that we have influence but not control. We are not puppet masters. Stuff happens. It's what we do in response to the "stuff" that defines who we are, our happiness level, and our "success" (however we choose to define that).

~ Assessing Your Current State ~

Conducting an interview with yourself hopefully brought forth some eye-opening observations about where you've traveled to this point in your life. Now it's time to assess where you are today. Today is really just a culmination of every yesterday: The decisions you made brought you to today. So, where are you? Let's investigate.

Describe your worldview as it is today. What do you believe about yourself and the world around you?

Now, give me three words and three words only, to summarize your state of mind right now. Not how you *wish it would be*; how it really *is* right at this very moment.

1.

2.

3.

I'm assuming something isn't quite right in your world or you wouldn't have been drawn to a book called "Stuck U."...am I right? Get really honest in this step or put this book down right now and come back to it when you're ready. There is no sense wasting your time by glossing over something that requires more of your effort in order to really work.

~ Sticks and Stones May Break My Bones, But Words Will Nearly Destroy Me ~

When we define ourselves in strict terms ("I'm a big picture guy," "I'm the rebellious type," "I'm indecisive," "I'm impulsive"), we limit our available responses to a given situation. The word "always" is inferred in such a definition. It IS, we ARE, as we describe it. Language is very powerful. I have a rule in my coaching work: Clients must agree to eliminate "always" and "never" and replace with "sometimes" in their vocabulary. Doing so opens our minds to possibilities. I find that when challenged, everyone can come up with an example of when they didn't do what they said they "always" do.

As an example, I have a client who described herself as an indecisive person. When I probed, I discovered that this wasn't the case. She gets up out of bed in the morning. She then chooses a long list of personal hygiene products/practices, chooses her clothing and which style to sport, selects her radio station favorites…the list goes on and on. All of these selections require decisions among an endless stream of choices. Is she really an indecisive person? Or, does she struggle to make *certain* decisions? When we realized that the latter was true, we tackled the particular triggers in those areas that made it tougher for her to be decisive in *those* areas.

If she had kept defining herself so narrowly, she would have likely continued to opt out of circumstances where she would have been asked to make decisions. Imagine how limiting her life would have been? Don't limit yourself or other people by defining them with those big blanketing statements. Challenge your assumptions and definitions. Ready to assess that?

What are the things that you say are "always" true about you?

When are they *not* true about you? When do you do something that doesn't fit that "always" category?

Notice anything about the places you are and aren't like that? In front of certain people? When you're at work versus at home? What differences you see?

When you figure out where you are displaying the characteristic that you want to do more of you can do more of it in other places. Isn't that great? We can start seeing that we already are where we wish to be, at least part of the way. We are just witnessing what we've always been. Our only error has been using the wrong words to define who we are and what we do. Yep. We are responsible for our own limitations. We are responsible for our own tethering to an existence that reduces our space in the world. "I'm impulsive" can serve to excuse certain reckless behaviors, but that's not the whole story. True, extreme impulsivity is dangerous (walking into traffic), so not many people are truly "impulsive" all of the time. They live within limits. They obey the law. They exist within a structure or myriad ones. They do act impulsively *at times.* At other times they don't. They live on a spectrum, venturing into the outer limits at times. All of us have the capacity to embody any behavior at any point on the spectrum. It is all about choice. Confidence. Intention. Risk.

We concluded that what you did yesterday (and all those other pesky yesterdays) got you to where you are today, so it follows that if you want to be someplace else in the future, you'll need to start making decisions that are consistent with that future vision of yourself. What *is* your future vision of yourself? Shall we get started with your vision of where and how you'd like to be? Without it you'll just be bouncing between the guardrails of life. First, we have to determine what you have control over and what you don't or you'll be aiming at the wrong targets.

~ Power & Control (Buckets) ~

"Experience is not what happens to you,
it's what you do with what happens to you." ~ Aldous Huxley

Power and control? Sounds pretty intriguing, doesn't it? Before you get too excited to read further, I'm talking about personal power (not dominion over others) and control buckets (that describe what you're in control of, what you can influence, and everything else). The great news is that you get to choose where you want to focus your energy. You're in charge of your thoughts, feelings, beliefs, and behaviors; basically, how you experience yourself and the world. What aren't you in charge of? Other people, their decisions, and actions. Once you get clear on the things you can control, on the things you can influence, and on all the things that are not under your control or influence, you have increased your personal power. You are drawing all of your power in one, harnessed direction instead of banging your head up against a wall trying to change things you can't change.

Are you feeling more powerful? No, it's not overpowering others, but rather it's about empowering yourself to reduce the unhealthy influence of others (and outside experiences). Where is your power? It's in you. You have more power than you have probably ever embraced. Why? Most likely because you have been scattering your power all over the place, worrying about things that you can't affect in the least, existing in relationships where you've handed over the reigns to other people instead of claiming your own priorities, needs, and influence. The world is not in charge of you, and neither is that inanimate object called "the world." You are. You are in control of you. No one else. Take your power and wield it. It's the only way things in your life are going to change for the better.

"Enduring hardship isn't just about strengthening one's character… it's about building one's testimony." ~ Jenny Lee Sulpizio

~ Assessing Your Risk Tolerance ~

"Leap, and the net will appear." ~ Zen saying

I hate black ice. I know it's wrong to hate, but I do. I hate it. Just the thought of it makes me tighten to my core. Actually, come to think of it, any kind of ice fills me with dread. I make jokes about it but it's not at all funny to me, to be honest. Just this morning I went out to shovel a wintry mix from my driveway and it took all of my resolution to stay out there and remove it. I walked with such hesitation you'd think I was risking my life. In my experience, I may just as well have been.

What the hell is wrong with me anyway? Well, too much to list here, but as it relates to my terror surrounding black ice: I fell on it on my driveway as I was taking out the trash about a year ago. The initial injury to my shoulder was searing pain like I've never known but that wasn't the worst of it. At all. I spent the next year battling pain, visiting various doctors, radiologists, physical therapists, and chiropractors trying to get some relief. From all reports, I dislocated it and this wasn't caught by a doctor, a radiologist, and two physical therapists over the course of seven months. Seven *months.* Well, that's only partially true. We pieced together that my shoulder was dislocated and was "re-located" after five months by my chiropractor who thought she was treating me for frozen shoulder.

Anyone who has ever suffered from a dislocated shoulder and/or frozen shoulder knows that this is a protracted recovery process. I was on massive doses of pain relievers and was most likely damaging my liver in the process. Even on the maximum dosage, I found it hard to stand up, walk, drive, or just function. My entire body fell apart in trying to compensate for the injury. My back, hips, left leg (it was my left arm), and neck were a source of constant pain. I had no energy for anything: Work, kids, volunteer stuff, self-care. I know it's shocking, but I gained weight (no gym visits for me and chocolate is quite the compassion giver). That just made me even more energetic (NOT) and full of joy (*please*).

Why did all of this happen? Black ice. Walking up my driveway to take the trash to the curb two days after Christmas. 'Tis the season to be injured, fa la la la la la la la la. What does my clumsy ordeal have to do with change and risk tolerance? Absolutely everything. We get conditioned, through our experiences, to expect certain outcomes. When I see ice (black or otherwise), I panic, seeing a year of agony ahead of me. Could I walk cautiously across it and suffer no injury whatsoever? You betcha. The problem is that my experience tells me that it's likely that I'm going to be devastated if I get anywhere near it. So, I avoid it at all costs.

If you've ever attempted to change something about yourself or your life it may not have gone so well. Maybe the weight you vowed to lose either wouldn't come off or came right back on? Perhaps you lost a friend as you stopped being who they knew you to be? Worse yet, you might have bragged about how things were going to be different this time and you fell flat on your face, changing nothing about you or your circumstances. You suffered public humiliation and you're aware that the people around you might not believe that this time will be different. Ever visit a fitness gym in the first few weeks of January? It's like a church on Christmas or Easter. Packed. The resolve that often accompanies New Year's resolutions often lasts a few weeks before life gets in the way and we get off track. So, you ask yourself, "How will this time be any different?" It can be quite different – and wholly successful – if you follow the path this book outlines for you, and part of that is coming to terms with your risk tolerance. Here's the singular question that you need to answer in order to gauge just how risk tolerant you are:

What are you willing to give up in order to experience change in your life?

Friends? Family? The safety of being predictable? Being seeing as loyal? Fitting in to the mold you've been occupying? The comfort of dysfunction and failure (or falling short of your potential)? It's not failure (or the fear of it) that holds most people in place, it's the pain that comes with success. I attended a meeting with a roomful of passionate, intelligent, independent women who were learning how to open the floodgates to their financial freedom. One woman courageously stood up to receive guidance from the group. She shared her fear that if she asked for the rate that she believed her services were worth that she would lose her husband (and therefore, her family) in the stir. Woman after woman stood up, affirming that only good things would come from her receiving the abundance she deserved, they urged her not to worry and to step forward into her success.

I'm not one to be quiet when I have an opinion or something to say that I feel needs to be said (shocking, right?), so I, too, stood up to share my support for this uneasy woman. My words were very different, though. I shared my story of loss, fractured friendships, and outright bullying behavior that I experienced when I showed up in my own life and claimed my abundance. I told her that she might, in fact, lose those she thought were friends. I assured her that her success would most assuredly come at a personal cost.

As I said to her then, I say to you now: Come to terms with the fact that you will see changes in your personal (and professional) relationships when you undergo a process of change. Insecure and jealous people will likely undermine, disparage, reject, and abandon you. They will become your haters. You are becoming a shining example of who they cannot or will not be and that mirror is painful for them. They will act on that pain and hurt you, intentionally or unintentionally. Darkness does not crave light, and people on the path to self-discovery and growth seek and emanate light. Your light threatens them.

My advice to you: Take an honest and thorough inventory of the key players in your life. Are they likely to react negatively if you start improving your circumstances? Are you okay leaving them behind? If risking those relationships is holding you back, I urge you to do some work on this before you pursue the change you're hoping to make or you'll suffer unexpectedly and unnecessarily.

You're reading this book to help you undergo a change in your life because you recognize that it's hard to do and you need support. There are many among us who don't have the confidence to start the process. Do you? Where is your confidence level?

~ Finding Your Roar ~

"Life shrinks or expands in proportion to one's courage." ~ Anais Nin

When we are fearful, we hesitate, we get stuck, we shrink back from life, from connections, from our potential, and from our very essence. Fear builds on fear. When we are fearful we attract what we seek, proving to ourselves that the world is a scary place and that we are right to mistrust it. We shrink away from conversations, experiences, and confrontations. We meet our need for control by staying stuck because at least we can control *that.* There is safety in staying stuck because the devil you know seems better than the devil you don't. Fear reinforces our distrust of new things, encouraging us to hold still and stay stuck in our sameness. It's the Fear-Trust-Control Model (see page 25) at play in our lives. (If you want to learn more about it, please check out *Feed The Need.*)

High fear equals low trust which promotes controlling behavior aimed at reducing our anxiety (that beautiful by-product of feeling a lack of trust and control and an abundance of fear). The only thing we can do to intervene (lessen fear, increase trust, decreasing controlling behaviors) is to work on building relationships. The most important relationship you'll ever have is with yourself so you're going to need to start there.

We often lack confidence, particularly in new and challenging situations. We can talk ourselves out of anything. We tell others our "reasons" for not acting. For pausing. For pondering. At the end of the day, these are all bullshit. They make up the bullshit narrative we tell ourselves that keeps us safely in the comfort of our stuckness. Yeah, yeah, the "reasons" are "real" and we *do* need to acknowledge them so that we meet our need for validation. After we've self-indulged in that space for a few minutes (not months or years, folks), it's time to move on. Setting fear aside gives you confidence, but do you know what builds *fierce* confidence? Moving right through that monster, saying "bring it!" as you go head first into the storm. Go *get* it.

~ Running Into Your Fear ~

"I learned that courage was not the absence of fear,
but the triumph over it. The brave man is not he who does not feel
afraid, but he who conquers that fear." ~ Nelson Mandela

I love thrift stores. I shop in them often because there are so many treasures in them. Think about it: In order to be in a thrift store, an item had to have been bought by someone already. The book section is the best because it's like a library of loved books that were released to be loved by the next person who picks up a volume. It was in the thrift store that I found, "Run To The Roar" by Paul Assaiante (2012). In this book, he offered a stunning perspective shift that forever changed the way I perceive our fight or flight instinct when faced with fear.

In the wild of the Sahara Desert, antelope are on constant watch for lions who wish to hunt them down. Lions have a very predictable hunting pattern. They encase the antelope herd between two points: A small den of strong, fast lions and the large, slow, dominant male. The dominant male roars loudly and the antelope run from him into the waiting lions' hungry and powerful jaws. If they had run toward the roaring male instead, it's most likely that they would have lived because the large lion was slow and couldn't catch them at full speed.

What's the lesson? When you run toward the roar (your fear) you actually face *less* danger. There is more danger in hesitating and running away than in heading straight toward your fear. If there is a proverbial monster under your bed, it's far better to introduce yourself to it and know what you're dealing with than leave it in the dark as a mystery. If you don't, it becomes larger than life and your vision of it is not very accurate. You can't fight what you can't see.

Besides, we were all born with a roar: Our first cry. "Pay attention to me and pay attention to me NOW!" Babies who score highest on the APGAR scale do so in part because of their boisterous roar. It came from passion for life. It also came from fear. Fear that if we were ignored we would literally die. Over time, it gets worked out of us. We get numbed down. Our roar is quieted. In order to claim the courage of a lion that has been in us all along, we have work to awaken it. We have to use our fear to motivate us. Fear is helpful because it motivates us to pay attention, to look around and look within.

You may come from fear or come from joy, but we all struggle with fear. Owning your voice is daunting. No one else has your voice. *You* have your voice. *You* must own it. No more hiding in the shadows. No more being complicit and compliant. If you live this way, imagine your "playback" of your life. Will you be proud? Will you have lived your talents? Your passions? Your TRUTH? A roar comes from the belly. It is power and passion. When we own our roar, we own our power. Sometimes when we grow up with fear, we develop anger instead, as rebellion. Are you ready to let that go?

In the movie "After Earth," Will Smith's character coaches his son to survive an enemy attack by dealing with his fear directly. The enemy is only able to kill him if he can smell his fear. In essence, fear will literally kill him. Will Smith's character says that fear is not real. Danger is real, but fear is a reaction to a possible future event, which is not real. The future event hasn't happened yet. It is a conjuring of the mind. Fear quickly transforms into anxiety which promotes panic. Panic can calcify you, and foster inaction. It can also throw you into a tizzy and encourage frenetic action without thoughtful pause. It can foster reactivity. Reactivity is action without power. Squirrels don't get promoted: Lions do.

Claiming personal power requires calm, centered intention and translates into a response, not a reaction. It's the difference between ping-pong and golf. Get the picture? See the difference in your mind's eye? In which game (ping-pong or golf) are you able to pause and strategize? In one, mastery is based on reaction time (ping-pong). In the other, mastery is based on strategy. We have more power when we can strategize and come from a place of calm passion. Here are some questions to stir up your roar.

What do you most want to roar about? Why?

Who do you want to hear your voice?

What situation(s) are waiting for to show off your roar?

What difference would it make?

Who do you know who roars? *What* do you know about him/her? *What meaning* do you make of their roar?

When we get to the Action step, refer back to these notes for possible changes you can make that will help you to claim your roar and change your life for the better.

"You see something scary, you should stand up and
step *toward* it, not away from it. Instinctively,
reflexively, in a raging fury." ~ Lee Child

~ Assessing Your Emotional Agility ~

"We can only be what we give ourselves the power to be." ~ Native American proverb

To review, **Emotional Agility equals high emotional competence mixed with high change-ability.** Emotional Agility answers the burning question of how change occurs: Through mastering emotional agility. When you can consciously choose your behavior, regardless of the circumstances, you are developing *emotional agility*. Emotional agility is key to health (emotional, psychological, physical, and spiritual) and inherently promotes success. The three pillars of emotional agility are:

1. **Insight**
2. **Distance-ability**
3. **Flexibility**

Where are you right now in terms of emotional agility? Let's address each pillar, one by one.

~ Insight ~

Some people seem to be *born* insightful. They can see past the noise of a situation and zero-in on what is *really* going on. They listen at a different, deeper level. They understand what's going on without hours and hours of interviews of every player. They just *get* it. How? Usually because they spend time getting to know themselves first. They develop an inner voice that assesses what they think and feel about things and creates a worldview and corresponding frameworks for solving problems that crop up. Having done this for themselves, they are apt to apply these strategies to other people in their lives. They can transfer their understanding of themselves to understanding others.

Sounds easy enough? Think again. A huge host of people confuse assumptions with insight. It's a fine, but critical, line. Assumptions are a short cut and based on *control.* Insight comes from a caring place, with value placed on *connection*, *validation*, and, in the end, *growth.* Assumptions put people into contrived boxes, often to serve the agenda of the person placing them there. Insight seeks to understand people and their motivations, to bring more connection.

How do you know if you're showing insight or promoting assumptions? The answer is in your intention. If your intention is to understand, to know, to gain truth, then you're on the insight track. If your intention is to check a box, to form an opinion, to be right, then you're on the assumption train. Let me be clear: You can have a negative insight about someone. You can perceive that someone is toxic, addicted, manipulative, narcissistic, or passive-aggressive. These insights are often based on experience and taking stock of how someone has been treating us over time. We notice things, we make mental notes, and we often discuss these pieces of information with others to "check them out." We build a mosaic with these tidbits, these insights.

Assumptions follow a very different path. Assumptions are quick-triggered. When we make assumptions we make them quickly and without checking them out. With assumptions, we are craving definition so that we can put someone into a box and leave them there. Assumptions are the hallmarks of prejudice and gossip. Assumptions hate inquiry; they love certainty so they don't want to find out if they are wrong. They want to be accepted on face value. That's the control shining through. Assumptions want everything defined so that things feel more settled and in control. And, you know what they say about when you ass-u-me something: It makes an "ass" out of "u" and "me." Clever, eh? My daughter's fifth grade teacher sent her home with that gem so I hear it all the time. Thanks, Mr. Quigley!

So, where do you find yourself more of the time? Making assumptions about people, or being insightful about them? Are you quick to judge, or do you slow down and try to connect with their experience, based on your own? Be honest. Is your intention to *understand* or to *judge*? Are you better about using your insight with certain people? How have you developed insight with yourself first? Do you know yourself? Are you in tune with what's going on your inner world? Only then can you use informed insight with the outer world.

~ Your Third Eye ~

Insight can be spurred by someone other than you. My job as a leadership consultant and coach is to be the "third eye" to individuals and organizations because, let's face it, we all have blind spots. We all have things we can't, or don't want to, see. We are too close to the situation, with vested interest in it turning out one way or another. When you use the perspective of an outsider, you gain a third eye. You can see things a little differently, and therefore act upon things differently. The more insightful and detached the third eye, the more beneficial he or she can be. When looking to recruit a third eye, ask yourself the following questions before you hire or engage them in your pursuit of change:

1. How much do they understand you and/or your organization?

2. How open are they with you about their observations? Do you get the truth or a sugar-coated version of it?

3. Do they seem to have a pony in the race, or are they wedded only to your growth and success?

If they do all three of these things, get them onboard with you as soon as possible. You need all the helpful eyes you can get.

~ Distance-ability ~

Yeah, I know, I made up this word. That's the super-amazing thing about writing your own books: You get to make up stuff! I like this term because it's very intuitive. Just by reading the word you know the skill I'm looking to train you in: The "ability" to "distance." What does the ability to distance look like? I'm so glad you asked!

Imagine you're looking at a tulip, holding it one inch from your face. What do you see? Color. Shape. Contour. Now, hold it at arm's length. What do you see? Looks different, doesn't it? That's perspective. Creating distance creates perspective. Now, imagine the most wretched, stinky bag of garbage you've ever smelled and then imagine that it's plopped right at your feet. You can't escape the stench. It's overwhelming and you're about to vomit. You can think of nothing else but the smell and you're trying to figure out how to get away from it as soon as humanly possible. Now, imagine that you're sent away from the horrid bag of nastiness and you go outside, with a glass door between you and the bag. Might you notice the color of the bag, its fullness, its contours, etc.? Why? Because, in both cases, you gained distance which facilitates perspective. When you have perspective, you are more perceptive. Being perceptive is just another way of demonstrating insight, the first pillar of Emotional Agility. Seeing the connections?

Let's get back to Distance-ability, shall we? If gaining distance promotes perspective, why do we care? Simple: Perspective equals power. No, I don't mean power over others. I mean personal power. When you have emotional distance and perspective you are more able to respond to the situation because your head and heart are working together instead of being reactive, where your emotions are in charge.

Think of a toddler. You can't reason with a three-year-old when they are hot, hungry, or tired because those conditions make them highly emotional (and reactive). Forget a three-year-old; you'd have a hard time reasoning with *me* under those conditions. Distance-ability allows you to step back and gain perspective; to use your powers of insight to hold your power in the situation.

Exercise: Stand up. Take a long, deep breath in, completely filling your lungs, and hold it. Feel the strength of that. As you exhale, imagine blowing out a table full of candles, slowly, confidently, purposefully. Now, start panting, taking quick, shallow breaths in and out. Getting lightheaded yet? Stop and return to your normal breathing pattern before you hurt yourself and sue me.

Why did I have you do that? I wanted you to experience the power of Distance-ability. The first breath piece – the strong, deep breathing – is what Distance-ability brings to you in terms of calm and focus. For those of you who have participated in yoga, breathing in this purposeful manner is a cornerstone of that regimen. The panting, well, that's when you're emotionally tangled up in a situation and anxiety, anger, confusion, etc. have taken over. You're directly caught up in the situation and you're having trouble catching your breath.

When you took that deep breath, could you feel your focus on your lungs and the space in and around you? In contrast, when you were panting, were you able to observe anything else in and around you? It was hard, wasn't it? Panting is an anxious state. Anxiety does not hold calm and peace and strength. Deep breathing does that. The next time you're anxious, focus on your breath, only your breath, and bring your strength back to you.

~ Creating Distance From Your Thoughts ~

"There are only two mistakes one can make along the road to truth: not going all the way, and not starting." ~ Buddha

There is a Buddhist practice wrapped up in mindfulness that goes something like this: You are not your thoughts. The thoughts that you think are not who you are, they are what you are doing; what you are allowing in to your consciousness. You are not them and they are not you. They are a "thing," just as you are not the hat you wear or the car you drive. In order to adopt this powerful way of thinking, you must create some perspective, some distance from your thoughts. You must be able to see them as conscious and unconscious reflections of your beliefs about and experiences of the world.

The next time you have a thought racing through your mind (or a cluster of them keeping you up at night), pause and start speaking to the thought as though it was the thought your best friend was having. Observe it ("Well, I see that this is the thought on tap right now"). Challenge it ("Does this really exist? Is it possible that this doesn't fit here?). Then, if it doesn't serve you, if it makes you more anxious or angry, let it go.

~ Flexibility ~

I didn't make up this term, but I am using creative license to apply it for my purposes in helping you along your change journey. I am defining Flexibility as "being able to think and behave differently in response to internal and external cues." In order to be flexible, insight helps, as does Distance-ability. It's hard to be able to behave differently if you cannot think (insight) differently or feel (distance/perspective) differently. Therefore, thoughts & behaviors lead to actions (*Insight* & *Distance-ability* lead to *Flexibility*).

Forming the foundation of Flexibility is the ability to recognize choice in thoughts and behavior: To see options. To not be wedded to sacred cows ("I always do it this way"). Put it this way: If you can't see that you even *have* choices in how you think and behave you won't be able to exercise those choices. Awareness of those choices is the "do not pass go, do not collect $200" stop-dead-in-your-tracks, you-must-get-this-step step. Awareness requires presence, presence requires focus, and focus requires calm. The good news? This kind of calm is powerful. With calm, you can exercise a wider range of choice and <u>those with more choice have more power.</u>

What does Flexibility look like in real-life situations? People with Flexibility don't automatically do things just because they did it that way before. If someone sits in their seat, they move to another seat. If plans change, they adapt to the new ones. When they are faced with a dilemma, they think through their options. They brainstorm. They don't react, they respond thoughtfully. They are good at pausing so that they can see the choices available. When it seems that they only have one choice, they investigate and challenge to unearth more choices. They aren't affixed to one solution, they entertain many possible solutions. They favor effectiveness over efficiency.

Now that you know what your intended outcome is – to enhance your emotional agility – it's time to continue to collect the resources to support your change journey by assessing what's going on outside of you.

~ Assessing The Landscape ~

"Stay close to anything that makes you glad you are alive." ~ Hafiz

Stuck U.

In this section, we are going to tackle the influencing factors that can either trip you up or support you in your change process. If you don't know the weather, you don't know what to pack. If you don't know what's going on around you, you don't know how to prepare. Remember what we said about acquiring personal power? It's all in being responsive (not reactive) and that requires calm preparation. Knowing what your triggers are and figuring out what the hardest step will be for you is critical in building your greatest personal power.

We've come again to one of those moments where I need to fess up and share my worldview with you because it forms the structure for the next segment of this book. I know, I know, I should have tipped my hand in the beginning of the book but it would have been out of place there. It's relevant here so it's time we got clear on it.

People are made up of bones, flesh, organs, cells, cartilage, and all sorts of liquids (and some gases, too). More than all of that, we are made of energy. Pure energy. There are those positive, happy, near-buoyant people that you come into contact with and all you want to do is let their energy build you up and lighten the space you're in. Blending your energy with theirs is the best decision you could make, so have at it.

Have you ever gotten near someone and chills ran up your spine? You were creeped out and wanted nothing more than to jet from the situation before you "caught" whatever they had. That's energy. Their ugly, toxic energy was emanating from them and reaching you, so much so that you were conscious of it and wanted to protect yourself from it blending with yours. You weren't conscious of that? Maybe next time you will be and you'll take more precautions to guard your energy from infiltration.

A client of mine walked into a building where he could literally *feel* the negative energy wash over him. It was suffocating. I wish I could report that he got into his bubble and hopped into observer role so that he could stay out of the ick, but I can't. He walked into the meeting he had and he was so off that he lost his temper on more than one occasion. He couldn't get out of that building fast enough.

When I later asked him about this train wreck of a meeting, he was able to go back to the moment when he was walking down the hall and felt oppressiveness all around him. He let it take over his mood and then he spewed it all over everyone he came into contact with moments later. What would have happened if he had been able to get some emotional perspective on this feeling he had instead of reacting to it?

If you eat rotten food, chances are, you're going to vomit. If you take in toxic energy, you're going to "vomit" it out, too, usually all over other people. What can you do? Don't consume it. Observe it. Comment on it. Maybe even try to shift it. But for goodness sake, don't let it become a part of you. Distance brings perspective. Perspective brings power. Want power? Let the negative energy be what it is and refuse to let it become a part of you.

What if it's positive energy? You want to soak that energy in like it's the air you breathe and the water you drink. Positive energy is life-affirming and promotes growth and pleasure, and there is a shortage of that in many areas of our lives. Have a savings or retirement account? Ever feel like you have too much money in it? Yeah, right. Positive energy is a lot like money; when you acquire it you can make more of it, and the more you have the more abundant you feel, yet, you have no desire to stop amassing it. And sharing it.

What does all of this have to do with the change process? Your greatest resource is energy. Energy is working to hold you in place, pull you backward, or propel you forward. As you discover where you are, and affirm where you want to be, you can start to see what will send you toward (and hold you from) your desired state. I call these two forces *constraining factors* and *energizing factors.*

Constraining Factors

These are the people, places, thoughts, and things that are bound to trip you up if you're not paying close attention. Their energy works against you, usually because they are focused on different things than you are. In the case of your thoughts, constraining factors are those that are working against you and your best interests, whether those thoughts are conscious or subconscious.

They might even refer to parts of you: Your attitude, your inner voice (critic), your negative thought patterns, your habits, your aspirations, and your lifestyle. Are you in a bad marriage? Is your spouse (or are you) an addict? Do you have a tendency to beat yourself up over every little thing you do wrong? Constraining factors can stall you completely or just slow you down a bit, depending on your level of awareness and preparation. In order to be prepared for them rearing their ugly heads, get clear on what they are.

List five constraining factors you need to attend to in order to really tackle the change process:

1.

2.

3.

4.

5.

Now, for each constraining factor, brainstorm some things you can do to *reduce their influence* in your change process. Perhaps you could shift your thinking about the importance of one of them. Or, you might be able to eliminate it altogether. Let's suppose one of them is a friend or family member or co-worker who is always criticizing or second guessing what you do. Maybe you could reduce the amount of time you spend with or listening to them. Get it? Ready? Go!

1.

2.

3.

4.

5.

We've looked at your walls so it's time to look at your doors. Ready?

Energizing Factors

These are the people, places, thoughts, and things that build you up and send you on the path to improving yourself, the wind beneath your wings. Their energy works for you because they are focused in the same (or similar) direction. In the case of your thoughts, energizing factors are those strengthening, positive, empowering thoughts that encourage you to move forward and take action. If your attitude is upbeat, your inner voice is generally supportive, your habits are not self-destructive, then you have energizing factors in your favor.

List five energizing factors you can focus on for strength in the change process:

1.

2.

3.

4.

5.

Now, for each energizing factor, brainstorm some things you can do to *increase their influence* in your change process. Perhaps you could give more credit to the importance of one of them. I'm guessing that one of them is a friend or family member or co-worker who is always supporting you and cheering you on. If so, you could increase the amount of time you spend with or listening to them. You know the drill. Get it? Ready? Go!

1.

2.

3.

4.

5.

~ Assessing Your Desired State ~

"As water takes whatever shape it is in,
so free may you be about who you become." ~ John O'Donohue

You're making amazing progress in this Assessment chapter, figuring out where you've been and where you find yourself now. It's time to set a vision for where you want to be in the future. What's your ideal vision of yourself? You know you don't want to be where you are right now, but where *do* you want to be? Do you have a clear image of it in your head? Can you describe it? Then, do it.

The first step is to get a 500 foot view of your life. It comes down to establishing a clear sense of your greater purpose so you can orient yourself to your North Star. What's your North Star? Where are you headed? What are you focusing on? What you focus on is where you go and what you attract, so set your sights on the right end point. Ever sail a boat? One *fraction* of one degree off and you'll end up in another country. Being crystal clear in your vision is super important to getting to where you want to be. So, where is that?

~ Setting a Strategic Vision for Your Life ~

"If you want something you've never had,
you'll have to do something you've never done." ~ J.D. Houston

What is your life's purpose? Why are you here? What do you want to accomplish? What do you want to leave as a legacy? How do you define "success?" You can't change what needs to be changed until you can identify where you want to go. Think of the most inspirational and instrumental people you've met or known of: What did they have in common? Countless leadership experts have tackled that question from a variety of angles and to a mixture of depths. For the purposes of this discussion, let's keep it simple. Above anything else they share a passion for a life purpose, even if they didn't articulate it that clearly.

For example, I imagine that Martin Luther King, Jr. would have said, "To create a world free of racial discrimination." Mother Teresa similarly would have said, "To bring God's love and support to the poor." And so they did. They could have done all sorts of things and made a litany of different decisions along their respective paths but they didn't. They stayed the course. And they realized their destinies. Because they created them. Through passion, commitment, decision making, and a clear focus on their life purpose. There's a saying that each of those people (and any other great like Albert Einstein or Michelangelo, etc.) had the very same number of hours in a day that each of us do. Perhaps some had extraordinary talent or intelligence, but many were born with bumps and bruises, challenges and gifts, just like you and me. What they grabbed onto with both hands was their *purpose.*

How do *you* define a life purpose? How do you know if you got it right? A true purpose will be the spring in your step, the twinkle in your eye, and the reason that when you get knocked down you are able to get back up. It's your motivation and your passion. In my experience, when you figure it out and share it out loud with someone, your voice is stronger and your posture is straighter. You are using your true voice.

What is your true essence? Why are you here? What do you want to be your legacy? What is the special energy you want to share with the world? Start sketching down some notes here. There's no time like the present to get you rolling.

"You rarely have time for everything you want in this life, so you need to make choices. And hopefully your choices can come from a deep sense of who you are." ~ Mister Rogers

~ Spectrum Surfing ~

Would you believe me if I told you that no qualities (aside from being evil, of course) are either all good or all bad? All qualities are on a spectrum, with any quality and its opposite holding the bookend positions on the spectrum. To illustrate what I mean, I'm hopping in my little time machine and bringing you back to a time when my job was to place candidates in jobs or I didn't make any money. No pressure there, right? One of my talents was in the interview prep. The core mission of the interview prep was to get a candidate in the most confident, clear, and poised position to nail an interview and get the job. I only got paid if my candidate got the job, and each job was worth up to a month's salary for me so I was *all* about the prep. What was the question that got them the most riled up and nervous? "What is your greatest weakness?"

Have you ever been asked that? It feels like a complete set-up, doesn't it? There you are, cruising along, making great conversation, killing it, then out rolls the "why shouldn't I hire you?" question. Who wants to share their deficits in the middle of trying to sell their talents? It's pretty hard to rattle me, at least for more than a hot minute, so this is one of my absolute favorite questions. I'm sick, I know. Let me tell you why before you judge me too harshly.

As I explained, every quality is on a spectrum: Suppose you're laid back. On the other end of the spectrum might be rigid. Laid back can work beautifully in a host of circumstances (keeping others calm, interacting with strangers, finding creative solutions). Rigid can also be the right thing for the job (balancing spreadsheets, building machines, transporting troops). In other words, it's about the fit (where and how a characteristic or behavior is applied). When an employer asks you what your weakness is, you can respond with, "I'm known for being pretty laid back which can come across as uninterested at times, so I'm working to communicate my investment in what's going on while still being the person on the team who keeps things calm and creative." Congratulations! You got the job!

"Usually when people are sad, they don't do anything.
They just cry over their condition. But when they get angry,
they bring about a change." ~ Malcom X

When I reframed it to show them that everything is on a spectrum of "good" and "bad" qualities, candidates were able to see that they could share a "weakness" as the manifestation of the very strength they were proud of. Being detail-oriented is seen as a strength; however, when your nose is in the weeds you have to remind yourself to observe the big picture. If you're a "people person," you might find yourself being chatty and not as productive. Whether or not a trait is a weakness or a strength is a matter of degree (how far in the extreme it is), its application and context (being perky at a funeral probably isn't a good fit), and its flexibility (how you can "surf" the spectrum of the quality from one end to the other, depending on when and how you need it).

Objects in motion tend to stay in motion. If you are trying to move along the spectrum, just moving is progress and helps create more progress. If you're shy and don't speak up in meetings, first try making non-verbal and slightly verbal signals (mmm, mmhmm, nods, facial gestures, etc.). It becomes easier to break the silence because you aren't really silent. Ask a friend to ask you questions as a prompt so you aren't moving into the talking realm on your own inertia. When you're at a noisy dinner table it's easier to speak. You may not be noticed, and you most likely won't be drawing all of the attention to you because you spoke out, breaking the silence. Noise is good like that.

Recognize that all qualities are on a spectrum and that you have choice in exhibiting any characteristic you find fitting, situation-dependent. In doing so, you have claimed your power over your thoughts, feelings, and behaviors simultaneously.

Imagine yourself headed into a contentious staff meeting. (Never, right? Hah!). In your experience, staying peaceful and calm is the key to success in these situations, so head into the meeting in that state. Pretty quickly you'll observe that there are a couple of outspoken people who are bulldozing everyone. You may be peaceful and calm but literally feel yourself moving, almost effortlessly toward firm and intense when those qualities better suit the situation. That's spectrum surfing. There's nothing wrong with calm and peaceful, just like there's nothing wrong with firm and intense. Your behavior is your choice. Choosing the best behavior for the situation brings you squarely into your personal power and makes you 1000 times more effective in whatever you're doing.

Being able to demonstrate a quality based on where it's needed and where it fits best opens up a world of options. People with options have more power because their patterns don't dictate what they must do next. They get to choose. And, we're back to Emotional Agility! See how it's all fitting together? Speaking of fitting together, the subject matter of my first book fits here perfectly: How the Assessment step *must* include determining if you're getting your needs met.

~ Needs Fed? ~

Human beings have four core needs that demand to be filled: Connection, control, validation, and passion. If you want a more in-depth discussion on these needs, please pick up my book, *Feed The Need.* Maybe one of the reasons you picked up this book is because one of your needs wasn't being met and that's the thing you wanted to change. Or, perhaps you've been avoiding making a change in your life because you're (consciously or subconsciously) afraid that you'll stop getting one of those needs met if you change course.

What is the pattern or trait that you are targeting to change?

How is it currently serving you? What needs are you filling with your current thoughts, feelings, and behaviors?

Can you identify another way to get those same needs met without continuing your current pattern or trait?

If you don't solve this dilemma, you'll have a strong reason to stay the same. For example, if you're in a bad relationship or dead-end job, you might be feeding your need for connection (as weak as that may be) and control: The devil you know is better than the devil you don't, right? If you don't figure out how to feed your need for connection you're apt to slide right back into that old, sour relationship just because it serves that need. The same goes for your need to feel safe (control). As another example, if you interrupt people and dominate conversations you might be feeding your need for control (of the conversation) or validation (for the things you're saying). If you don't find a way to either feel more in control and validated in other ways (or surrender and accept that you may need to dial it down a bit on the need-o-meter), you'll fall right back into your old habits.

~ Giving Up Tolerations ~

"What you get by achieving your goals is not as important as what you *become* by achieving your goals." ~ Henry David Thoreau

There's a term in the coaching profession called "tolerations" which refers to things that you are putting up with that aren't serving your greater good. What are you tolerating in your life that if you stopped tolerating it, your life would be easier or better? This could be anything from being taken for granted in a professional or personal relationship to a cluttered desk. It's anything that is getting in the way of your success and happiness. At their core, tolerations are distractions and they make it harder for us to tackle the bigger things in our lives. They keep us in the weeds, pinned down to the life we've been living that hasn't been working so well for us. In order to give them up, we need to assess what they are. Activity time!

You probably tolerate things all over the place all of the time if you're like most people. In order to get your list together, it's important to understand the places tolerations usually show up. I break them down into three areas:

1. Physical (diet, exercise, self-care, dress)
2. Interpersonal (relationships with co-workers, bosses, friends, family, lovers)
3. Structural (clutter, disorganization, being "busy," lack of focus)

It's your time now to brainstorm. Next to each heading below, think about the things that you have in your life right now that each time you consider them they give you anything from discomfort to dread. Maybe it's that pile of papers in the corner of your office that beckons you every time you enter or exit the room. Perhaps it's that friend you get together with for coffee but you have absolutely nothing in common and feel like you just spent two hours you'll never get back as soon as you leave her. Or, it could be that extra 15 (or 20 or 50 or 70) pounds hanging around your mid-section (or backside).

Now is the time to get super honest and get it all out on paper. You have to face the truth to change it. Don't worry, though. We're still in the assessment phase so you have some time to figure out if anything on this list is going to make it to the chopping block. I'll bet that you have at least one in each area, and you might have a long list in one or more areas. Write. Pause. Review. Write again. Share with a trusted colleague or friend. Write again. Ready?

Physical

Interpersonal

Structural

Was there one area (physical, interpersonal, structural) that had more of your tolerations than another? If you could only pick one toleration to lift right now, which one would it be and why? I've seen clients make a list like this and start tackling them one by one like a maniac (and I mean that in a good way). Other clients (with other lists), start chipping away at them, one by one. Do what makes sense given your list. For now, since we are in the Assessment chapter, put a star next to the ones that you plan to tackle first and refer back to this page when we get into Action.

~ Setting Your Sights ~

"The way to get started is to quit talking
and begin doing." ~ Walt Disney

We've all heard rags to riches stories, of the guy in the mailroom becoming the CEO. We've also seen trust fund babies crash and burn in their lives, throwing away every opportunity in some adolescent rebellion turned train wreck. What do they both have in common? They both demonstrate that things are not predetermined. You can become whatever you imagine. It requires vision and confidence and a willingness to let go of past events, relationships, thoughts, and behaviors that no longer serve you.

What you believe about yourself you will attract more of into your life. You will draw to yourself that which you think you deserve. Making the decision to set your gaze on positive, abundant sights takes courage, a leap of faith, and a comfort with the unknown and with change.

How do you figure out if you're on the right track for getting the life you want? How do you know if you're focusing on the right trait(s)? What if, for example, you like being stubborn and you're not entirely sure you want to risk being wishy-washy? This section is going to show you how to tackle those important questions so you end up in the best possible place, and enjoy the view along the way. I'm going to show you how to close the gap. What do I mean by gap?

The gap is the difference between where we will experience optimal joy and fulfillment and where we are. It's not about changing who we are or major overhauls: It's about moving along the spectrum, through a series of simple steps and corrections. In closing the gap, we find (and practice) mindfulness, presence, positivity, and attentiveness. There are three main discussions we need to have in order to sketch out the roadmap you need to get to where you want to be.

1. **Characteristics Gap**: Where you are vs where you want to be on any given *characteristic.*
2. **Results Gap:** Where you are vs where you want to be on a *larger scale* (happiness, job satisfaction, success, etc.).
3. **Expectations vs. Reality Gap:** The *difference between expectations and reality* of any given situation, person, or experience.

You attract and find what you seek and focus on: Tragically and beautifully, for the bad and for the good. Understanding which gap to focus your efforts on is critical in getting to the right end point.

~ Characteristics Gap ~

This gap answers the question: Where you *are* vs where you *want to be* on any given characteristic? Are you one end of the spectrum (lazier than a dog vs. a productivity genius) or are you in a moderate place (sometimes on each end or moderate all of the time)? This gap tells you how far you have to shift in order to embody the characteristic you desire. It also gives you some insight into how much push back you'll receive from those around you. If you've always been irresponsible and flighty and now you're set to be Mr. Responsible and on top of everything, people are likely to notice. Heck, forget notice. They are likely to be in shock.

You'll have to be prepared for their reactions or their responses might throw you off track. Off track is *not* where you want to be. If you recall our discussion in the last chapter about finding places that you demonstrate a certain characteristic so that you can display it everywhere you want, you may be making the connection to this section. That depicts the Characteristics Gap: Where you're *currently* sharing and exploring it versus where you *want to be* sharing and exploring it. If you've been able to display the characteristic in certain circumstances but not others, your Characteristics Gap is not so big since you already have the tools to "be" that way.

~ Results Gap ~

This gap answers the question: Where you *are* versus where you *want to be* on an outcome basis (happiness, job satisfaction, success, etc.)? Are you absolutely miserable or just a bit blah? Have you lost job after job or are you just not excelling to your full potential professionally? Is your company about to go under or are you just not maximizing profitability? This gap tells you how hard you're going to have to work to get to where you want to be. There is no success without work so suck it up, Buttercup. If you've been settling for less than positive results you might have to dust the cobwebs out of your own head to adjust a new reality. If you've been struggling financially and you're slowly creating more financial abundance, you might need to let go of the fear you've held of going bankrupt if you step out for a pricey cup of coffee.

As an example, how are you with delegation? I've watched so many of my clients struggle with delegating tasks to their employees and stress themselves out in the process. Do you know what I told them to do? Imagine that they delivered the project that they were delegating wrapped in $100 bills. (Don't *do* it, Rockefeller, just *imagine* it.) Why? In order to communicate to yourself that they profit from completing that project. In more cases than not, they have a payoff, too. Offer it to them. You don't have to delegate every last thing; pick one or two components and see how they do. Remember: Baby steps close the gaps.

~ Expectations vs. Reality Gap ~

This gap answers the question: What is the difference between *expectations* and *reality* of any given situation, person, and experience? Are your expectations far from the reality of the situation, person, or yourself? Are you constantly disappointed? Or, does it depend on the person or circumstance? Do you have magical thinking or are you grounded in harsh reality? Can you easily accept what is real versus what you want or do you usually confuse hope with good sense? Do you trust people or situations before fact-checking? Reducing the difference between what you're expecting from yourself, others, and situations and what you are likely to experience (reality) will make you far more effective, calm, and successful.

As you can see, these gaps can run the gamut. What matters is how you use your characteristics, if your results are positive, how close your expectations are to reality, and that you observe and attend to these gaps with a high level of consciousness and proactivity. The gap between where you are and where you want to be is simply a series of steps and corrections. When you identify the source of your pain you can work to ease it. In the Action chapter, I'll introduce a concept I call "Power Shifting" which will demonstrate how you close these gaps. In the meantime…

~ Let's Get Real ~

How long do you have left on this planet? What? You don't know? It's not an indefinite amount of time? You mean wasted time is just that…wasted time? Please forgive my sarcasm. I'm using it to make a point that you don't have an endless (or even very lengthy) amount of time to have the life you say you want. You just don't. Healthy or not, you've got a discrete number of years and you have no guarantees on when this circus ends. My parents didn't make it out of their sixties; my father died in his mid-40s. You have stories of loved ones who died "too young," I'm sure. At some level, isn't *any* age "too young?" There is so much to see, do, and contribute here, how can we possibly fit it into 100 years, let alone *less.*

My parents left an imprint on this world, but imagine the power they could have had if they'd had longer? Better yet: What if they'd used the time more wisely? What if they'd shifted one proverbial inch to the right or left? How many lives could they have affected positively if they had harnessed their personal power and pledged to improve themselves ever so slightly? If each year they had tackled one quality about themselves that needed to change and just shifted it a bit? The overall shift would have left them almost unrecognizable, and most certainly with a longer time above ground.

~ Concluding Thoughts ~

If you don't know where you've been or where you are, you have no business making a plan for where you're going. You need to know how you got to this point or you'll miss some crucial information about yourself and how to avoid ending up back in this stuck state again. Companies (and individuals) who jump right into Action without spending some time on Assessment regret it in the short- and long-term. You need a plan of action in order to execute responsible and effective action.

Want more Emotional Agility? In order to get more of anything or better at anything, you need to figure out where you're starting from. If you glazed over the exercises in this chapter, I urge you to return to them and give them your time and attention. When you want something, you have to work for it, and this change process is no exception. Olympic medalists don't just walk into their event fresh off the sofa. You want easy? Put this book down until you're ready for a little challenge and hard work. This next chapter is about Action. Just reading about it doesn't count: You've got to be ready to put it into motion, sooner rather than later. You didn't get stuck in a day and you're not going to get unstuck in a day either. I'm good, but even I'm not *that* good.

(Now, where did I put my magic wand…..?)

Key Chapter Concepts

- To change, you need to take a long, hard look at yourself.
- Assessing your relationship contracts helps to right your expectations. When expectations and reality are far apart, disappointment reigns.
- Assessing lessons from the past helps to unleash your potential.
- How you speak & think about yourself creates your reality.
- Emotional Agility = Insight, Distance-Ability, & Flexibility.
- Energizing & Constraining Factors affect your change agenda.
- Identifying the gaps (Characteristics, Results, Expectations) creates a roadmap for change.

"All the art of living lies in the fine mingling of letting go and holding on." ~ *Havelock Ellis*

ACTION

"The secret to getting ahead is getting started." ~ Agatha Christie

~ Introduction ~

So many of us are afraid to act, afraid of the BIG steps necessary to get where we vision ourselves to be. In response to the fear, we stand still. If we took the little steps, made the small but powerful shifts in the things we think, say, and do, we would be *transformed.* Our cells changeover completely every seven years. It doesn't happen overnight. We don't SEE that change happening. Yet, it happens. What can you learn from this? Don't just stand there, DO something. Try something different. Shift your thinking or your behavior just a millimeter. The only one in charge of changing you is YOU. Thought changes can create behavior changes with discipline and habit formation.

Take the keys and make it happen. No one else is going to do it for you. The only way to prove to yourself that you can do things is to DO THINGS. Sometimes you can't wait to believe before you act. Act then you will believe. Or, you may never move from the place where you are.

Seems easy enough, right? How does this work, exactly?

We've already discussed that your thoughts build the pathway to your feelings which then trigger your behaviors. So, how do you behave differently if your beliefs aren't where they need to be? Think of it like this: When you try a new recipe, it isn't guaranteed that you'll like it but you get hungry as you cook anyway. If you want to make a change in your life, find a thought that matches the feeling you want and the behavior you seek. DO that. Not just once. Repeat it over and over. Keep trying until the thoughts you're thinking shift into the beliefs you're holding. You've already completed the awareness step and holding onto that awareness as you implement a shift in your thoughts is the main ingredient for success. In this chapter about Action, we will explore how you act upon changing your thoughts, feelings, and behaviors. Before we dive into each of those separately, we are going to have a general discussion about action itself. Ready?

The Cold, Hard Truth

"When you've got something to prove,
there is nothing greater than a challenge." ~ Terry Bradshaw

You have to want it. Your mother can't want it for you and make it happen. Your spouse can't have his/her heart set on it and it'll come to fruition. Your best friend can't give you stellar advice and thousands of encouraging texts and see you get unstuck. Your boss can't slam you up one side and down the other and just about show you the door and then sit back and watch as you transform yourself. YOU have to want it. This is the Action step, where your words stop meaning much of anything. It's all in the movement. It's the "put up or shut up" step. I really don't care how many people and situations have shown you that it's the right decision to change some thing or things about yourself. You might as well build your financial plan on a stack of scratch tickets. Sure, there's a chance that all that nagging and encouragement might shake you loose at some point. But, at the end of the day, you still have to scratch the dang ticket yourself. You. Just you. Now that we've gotten that out of the way, let's get you moving.

To make the changes to your life that you envision, you need to employ a practice I call "Power Shifting." Power Shifting is a conscious, deliberate movement toward the point on the spectrum at which you wish to exist. To Power Shift you must be able to see the differential between where you are and where you want to be *and* focus your personal power toward accomplishing that. It's an intense, solitary focus. For most people, your self-concept (and sense of the world around you) has been standing in the way of your potential. In order to make positive changes, you need to shift these; from fear to joy, from lack to abundance, and from suspicion to understanding, to name a few.

There are a million different ways to think of "action" but here is one: Tsunamis. Too much power for you to contemplate? Okay, how about an earthquake? That's some action if I've ever seen any! People tend to get at least a tad bit emotional when the topic of earthquakes comes up, especially if you or someone you know has lived through one. The media is so exhaustive in its reporting these days that even if you haven't actually felt the ground shake beneath your feet you may still feel traumatized by the images you've witnessed on the news. They can wreak havoc and cause damage, injury, and death.

So, why am I kicking off the Action chapter in a book about change discussing earthquakes? It's simple, really; earthquakes are a beautiful analogy to the change process and more specifically, the Action step. Have I piqued your curiosity? Bringing it down to basics, what exactly is an earthquake anyway? It comes right down to seismic shifts.

~ Seismic Shifts ~

Earthquakes are caused by a sudden and powerful release of energy from the Earth's crust which results in seismic waves that cause the rolling and shaking that we feel for miles from the epicenter (where the energy was released from). Since I'm no scientist, and if you ask my science teachers I wasn't even a very good student, I'm putting this in simple terms. Earthquakes represent change. Earthquakes happen when energy is released from the Earth. Change results from energy focused in a particular direction. Earthquakes cause ripple effects far from where the energy was released. Changes cause other changes and don't isolate themselves to the person or event that shifted.

The incremental shifts in our consciousness, in our awareness, in our tactics, in our perceptions, in our actions…become powerful. Like the butterfly effect. Most people have heard of the butterfly effect but most don't know how it came to be. Back in the early 1960s, a scientist was using a computer model to study the weather and he entered a number to the third decimal point instead of the sixth which completely changed the weather scenario. An analogy for this emerged, stating that hypothetically that if a butterfly flapped its wings it would create minute changes in the atmosphere that could affect a tornado's path. In effect, it's a domino effect of one little shift that promotes another which promotes another and so on.

What's the lesson here? Make a little shift, it might even be imperceptible, and watch nature take its course. A woman I knew once said that life is made up of seconds and inches: You can avoid an accident, meet a friend, win on a scratch lottery ticket, all with just a second or two alteration in your routine.

The things you've been doing all along that got you to this stuck place aren't necessarily all bad. They got you this far. Imagine you were fired without cause because of a political mess that you got caught in the middle of at your last job. You probably have some fear that you'll end up in the same mess again. Good for you. Of course you are. Don't talk yourself out of that. It's real and reasonable. If you tell yourself differently, you'll make yourself feel crazy and you won't trust the empty words of reassurance you're telling yourself.

Think about it: To NOT fear that would be insanity. It's happened and you have evidence to prove it. It doesn't have to drive your life, but it is perfectly appropriate for you to consider it. Now, you just need to shift a little to the left or a little to the right. Make small, incremental steps to move in another direction. Small shifts translate into seismic ones, so challenge yourself to do one a day. Start with the first one that presents itself to you. Don't try to blow the trait out of the water on the first day; pay it homage for how it's served you and then move gently away from it.

~ Baby Steps ~

"You put one foot in front of the other and soon you'll be walking out the door." ~ Maury Laws & Jules Bass

Often, because we are intimidated by the giant leaps in front of us, we resist change altogether. Instead, if we made a small movement, did one little thing differently, we would be in a new world of our own creation in no time at all.

We think tend to think that HUGE changes are necessary to turn our worlds around. It's typically just small, consistent changes over time. What would one small change look like? Back in the Assessment step, you wrote down a list of tolerations, right? If you didn't, here's your chance to go back there and do the work. Take the 30 minutes it'll take you to identify the things…the little crap…that are holding you back from opening up your pipeline of awesome.

Now what?

~ Baby Steps Method~

1. Identify the reason "it" bothers you (your "why").
2. State what would be different if you addressed "it."
3. Describe what addressing "it" looks like (What are the steps?).
4. If "it" is a small task (a few hours or less), tackle it in 30 minute chunks. Set a timer and stop after 25 minutes, cleaning up (closing out) whatever is left for next time.
5. If "it" is a habit to break (or start), take it one day at a time, rewarding yourself after each day you succeed.

Example: Let's suppose one of the things you wrote down was "cleaning up my desk." I've seen some desks that look like they jumped right out of an episode of Hoarders™. I'm going to assume that since you're still employed, yours is probably one or two notches down on the dial from that. How can you use the "Baby Steps" method to get this tackled without spending a Saturday at the office?

One pile at a time, that's how. Pick the easiest pile first. Maybe there is a stack of professional magazines teetering dangerously off the side of your desk. Set a timer for 15 minutes. Take the first minute to set your sorting criteria. Maybe it's "Anything over 6 months goes in the trash; I get to keep three magazines." Grab that stack and put it on another clear surface, maybe on an empty chair? One by one, scan the covers. See if there is something you really *must* read, something that will make your life better. Be critical. Recognize that an hour spent on a magazine is an hour not spent on something else. You can't make time, only spend it. Spend it wisely. Be a harsh judge on anything that will use the most precious resource you have: Time.

To all you leaders out there: If you want others to walk the walk, you have to talk it *and* walk it first and consistently. When you implement the tools in this book, you have the opportunity to create a language and behavior shift. In order to have that, you have to *model* it. In your meetings and communications with your team, you need to use the terms and phrases and models you've learned in this book to create a common language between you. Cultures have certain catch phrases and dialects that they use to create a sense of inclusion and belonging with their members. Organizations are the same. When you create that common language, you build a culture focused on enhancing emotional agility and leading you toward your best possible existence. That's a baby step that will have you running in no time.

So, what can you do today? Do one small thing differently. If you are fearful, take one step toward courage. If you are brash and bulldozing people, consider pausing and processing, considering what you could lose if you act in that moment. How do you eat an elephant? One bite at a time. How can you change the course of your life? Baby steps.

~ Setting the Stage for Failure ~

The first and easiest way we can set up ourselves for failure is by having expectations that are out of whack. If you expect yourself to not behave in concert with your prior experiences, you won't take the proper steps to shift away from those habits. To build new habits you need to first accept yourself where you are. Remember our discussion in Acceptance? Review it if you need to; it's critical. When you're disappointed in yourself and you let yourself fester there, that's a downhill slide to giving up on yourself and the new practices you're attempting. Don't start that slide.

"It's not what you do once in a while, it's what you do
day in and day out that makes the difference." ~ Jenny Craig

~ Knock It Off ~

The Universe doesn't like to be wrestled with, nor does it appreciate someone who chooses to let other people and circumstances run right over them. This life doesn't allow for…it *demands* your active participation in it. You can have your bad moments. You're human and it's expected that you aren't always going to be bringing you're A-game. Wallowing in it is another thing altogether. Act upon the world so that it can follow your lead. When you let it act upon you, you're bound to feel oppressed. Ain't nobody got time for that. Literally. Stop wasting time by being Mr. Nice Guy (or Ms. Nice Gal) and start behaving as though you're the captain of your own ship. News flash: You *are*.

I'm about to get "yell-y" (for those who haven't heard my kooky manner of speaking, I often add a "y" to the end of a word to make an instant adverb, hence "yell" becomes "yell-y"). When was the last time you got into your car on the passenger side and miraculously found yourself not going anywhere you wanted to go? Big shocker, right? Yet, I see so many people sitting in the passenger seat in their own lives and getting ticked off about being stuck somewhere they aren't happy about. Duh. You're not running your own life! You're letting other people run it for you. Feels pretty pathetic, doesn't it?

Maybe it's your parents or your spouse or some collective group of "people" who you think are expecting you to be a certain way. You've handed over the keys to your own life. What the heck are you doing that for? It's your life, for crying out loud! Live the damn thing! I've got my own life to worry about so please don't think I've got time to live yours, too. No one else has the time or the energy to actually live your life to its limits either, so stop checking out of your responsibility to live *your* life *your* way.

Don't believe me? Or is it that you just don't *want* to believe me? What if you just entertained the crazy woman writing this book and opened yourself up to the possibility that *you* are in charge and *you* can change your path by becoming aware of your own, unique potential. Make no mistake about it: When you change your way of *thinking* you can change your way of *doing*.

Anything is possible with passion. Okay, maybe not pigs flying but I'll bet that you could chuck one of those suckers pretty far and make it look like it was flying for a second if you were passionate enough about it to try it. (Folks, please don't visit a farm and actually do this...I'm speaking in euphemisms; get a grip). The Action step and getting yourself unstuck is supercharged when you've got passion.

~ Change in Organizations ~

One of the questions I get a lot in my work with corporations is whether or not change is possible? Can an organization really change its culture and its practices? If you've spent any amount of time in a company you've undoubtedly heard people say dismissive things like, "good luck getting that to change. That's just the way we do that around here." Have you ever heard of the "sacred cow?" In cultural terms it references the treasured importance of cows in the Hindu religion. In organizational terms, it refers to the practice of doing things for no reason other than that's the way they've always been done. To question the utility of the "sacred cow" is blasphemous. Employees give up on things being different, even if they operate to some extent in the spirit of change.

What distinguishes an organization that is poised for change from one that is likely to stay stuck? If your kneejerk reaction is "a pricey consultant," I thank you (and my contact information is in the back of this book). There is some truth to that, but that's just a piece of evidence of the organization's resolve to get unstuck. Companies that are successful in changing have these things in common:

- The leadership sends a clear message in word and in deed that change is necessary.
- Efforts at change, even with missteps, are rewarded openly.
- Internal and external resources (here's where a consultant like me jumps in) are harnessed to support and monitor the change.
- Open conversations about the change and its progress are encouraged.
- Leadership recognizes the power of the system to keep the organization stuck and takes deliberate actions to respond to those trigger points.

What does each item in that list have in common? That bothersome thing called being part of a system.

~ Power of the System ~

Power of the system? What does that mean exactly? The system is greater than the sum of its parts. Systems are their own entity, beyond the individuals themselves. Systems, or groups of connected individuals, have attributes that may be shared by the individuals but also may be somewhat distinct. Corporate culture is a good example. The culture of Company A may be "do whatever you have to do get ahead, either overtly or covertly." The employees may not exhibit those behaviors at home, but those behaviors are rewarded in the workplace.

In other words, a company is comprised of the individuals but it also has its own identity. As a system, there are rules about who does what and how they do it. There are power dynamics and struggles. There are roles that people fill, regardless of whether they may do so consciously. The system's "set-point" (homeostasis or center) holds it in place, keeping operations consistent and predictable. The system resists change. When people in the system try to change elements of it, forces within the system seek to hold the status quo. Maybe you're not reading this with work in mind. This same inventory can be applied to your family, friendship circle, or community. It's time to inventory.

What do you know about your group/organization's culture? What words or themes describe it?

What are some of the "rules of engagement" with members? What are employees supposed to do when they interact with one another? Is it the "in thing" to hate their jobs, complain about too much work? Are the rules rigid or flexible?

Who holds the power? In companies there are formal positions of power (vice president, director, etc.) but usually there are others in the organization who truly hold the power (of information, access, resources, etc.). How can you tell who is in charge?

What are the roles that people play? Again, I'm not referring to formal roles, I'm referring to things like, "information carrier," "bad news deliverer," "dreamer," and "realist." How does this work or not work?

How open are members about discussing these things listed above?
How aware are members that these things even exist?

In order to effect change on your system, you need to know where to exert your effort. Awareness is the first and most critical step, as you know. Accepting that an organization is where and how it is becomes the next logical step. The above questions constitute the Assessment. What do you do in the Action step? First and foremost, you need to bring the organization, particularly key leadership, through this Awareness, Acceptance, and Assessment process. In the Action step, based on what you learned through the Assessment process, you need to apply the facets of Emotional Agility to the organization: Insight, Distance-Ability, and Flexibility. Making those principles part of the culture is an imperative. The organization must also reward people when they display them and lead others using them. If you need help, you know where to find me.

~ Making Your Inner Critic Your Bestie ~

"We can complain because rose bushes have thorns,
or rejoice because thorn bushes have roses." ~ Abraham Lincoln

Failure happens. *Often.* I was once told I was the worst coach ever for suggesting that my client agree with the voice in his head that was telling him he could fail. Sounds pretty inspiring, doesn't it? I agree that it sounds pretty terrible at first but it's quite practical. Most people I've spoken with have a hefty amount of self-doubt they are wrestling with, sometimes to the point of immobilization or repeated failures. There is a familiar circle of self-doubt that most of us are ensnared in.

We don't believe in ourselves so we don't act (or we stumble when we do).

When we don't succeed, we have reason to believe that we are not worthy of success or happiness. We tell ourselves, "I failed so I'm a failure." In organizations, members say, "This place is a madhouse; it's hopeless." It becomes the chicken or the egg construct: Which came first? Our (self-) doubt, or the failures that prove it to be reasonable? Either way, we give doubt and insecurities such power over us that we may stop seeing success as an option. We hand over the keys to our lives to our inner critics.

What would happen if we made friends with our inner critic? Instead of seeing it as the enemy, we saw it as a trusted advisor. What if we acknowledged that our inner critic is just looking for safety and validation; to be seen as "right." In doing so, we would stop the fight. If our inner critic has been proven right in the past (it doubted us and we did, in fact, fail), it's not at all convinced when we drink from the well of positivity and affirmations that we can "do it."

In fact, when we invest our energy in all of the positive thinking mumbo jumbo we are declaring war on our inner critic, calling it "wrong" (gasp). Yeah, that never works. Why? Well, what do you do when someone tells you you're wrong when you have a proven track record of being right? Even more damning, you've been told you were wrong and still ended up being right? Would you argue? Fight for air time? You bet your sweet ass you would. You'd be doing the mental equivalent of tug-of-war, hell bent on proving you're right (again).

This is where making friends with our inner critic comes in. Friendship relies on trust. Trust is broken by lies and saying one thing and doing another. When we say we believe one thing (that we are going to succeed) but our actions and results prove otherwise (that we really believe that we will fail, and we do), we are breaking trust with our inner critic (who, if you haven't caught on by now, is the biggest player in your subconscious). Do you want to build trust with your inner critic? Focus on accepting that the inner critic may, in fact, be right to doubt you.

You don't need to stop there and just accept failure. On the contrary. Like any good friend would do, build trust by making attempts to avoid the failure, recognizing that it may happen. Have a game plan in case you fail. Ask yourself, "what's the worst that could happen?" and create a disaster relief plan for that outcome. Your inner critic will feel heard and safer, knowing that you're not ignoring the possibility that you could really mess this all up. It stops the fight. Instead of the tug-of-war to prove its point, you've created a partnership, a collaboration of sorts, to navigate the bumpy road from here to success.

Bottom line: How we speak to ourselves ends up being how we speak to others. If you disagree with that, know this: Even if you don't follow that straight line, what you're communicating to others with your energy and attitude **is** "speaking." You can immediately recognize people who feel like crap about themselves. They might as well wear a flashing light above their heads. Do you want to be seen as pathetic and miserable? I hope not. There are enough sad sacks out there without you joining them. Instead, exude positive and confident energy and it will, as sure as the sun will rise, return to you in spades.

~ The Universe is a Chick ~

Historically, people have referred to their god, whatever they may call their god, as a "he" as if he's a dude. Some of those progressive (and feminist) among us have shifted this and begun to speak of god as "she." I'm not going to take a position on this because this isn't a religious book and I don't want to start an argument that I'll most likely lose since you can just put this book down and I've lost you. That will make me sad and I don't like being sad. Instead, I am going to take save the danger of a knock-down, drag-it-out fight with you and risk making this pronouncement: The Universe is a chick. Let me explain.

A friend of mine has been struggling for years in every way imaginable: Socially, professionally, financially, physically, emotionally, mentally, you name it. She works hard and she loves hard. If she got in a ring, I'm pretty sure she'd beat the crap out of Evander Holyfield. Not too long ago, the Universe had served up a doozy to her and she contacted me for my advice. She was mad; terribly mad. She was ticked at herself for getting into yet another jam that she had no clue how to get out of. She was mad at the Universe for presenting her with this circumstance (once again). I gave her permission to be mad at herself and the Universe; to yell and scream and stomp around her house like a three-year-old. For a minute. Maybe ten. She needed to get all that garbage out of her system so she could take hold of my real advice which she couldn't hear if she was all pissy and raging.

Like so many of us who try to practice manifestation, or the habit of attracting things into our lives that we want, we make the mistake of demanding things to come into being in our time, in our way, on our terms. Unfortunately, the Universe does not like to be wrestled with. The Universe understands all of our human emotions but it doesn't like being told that we know best what we want, *when* we want it, and order up *how* it should show up in our lives. It likes to be danced with, spoken gently and peacefully to, and cuddled. Like a chick. The Universe is a chick. I rest my case.

Now, light some candles, pour some wine, bring yourself to a loving, accepting, and nurturing space and then begin visioning what you want to have present in your life. There are entire books and certification series on this stuff, people, so I can't possibly cover it to its greatest depth here, but it doesn't have to be too complicated to work. I've witnessed it over the years countless times. In resisting the urge to force your will upon the Universe, instead giving it permission to bring you the things you seek in the manner in which *she* decides, you'll reap bounty and get yourself unstuck from the limitations that you've set on yourself all of these years. Sounds pretty good, right?

~ Can't Fix Crazy ~

You can't fix crazy. Well, I suppose you can *try*. Lord knows I did for a good long time. I'm still known to get sucked into its vortex every now and again. Its pull is so very powerful. When we see it, and can actually recognize it as crazy, something in us wants to fix it. We want to be right, even though we never will be. Think about it: Imagine yourself arguing with a completely inebriated person. I don't mean a person with a healthy buzz. I mean a stumbling, slurring drunk. That never goes well. Why? Because they don't have a firm hold on reality or reason. Crazy people (or people acting in crazy ways) don't either.

When you start arguing with a crazy person and you use reason, you can end up feeling crazy because reason doesn't work on a crazy person. Crazy always wins. You're on the wrong battlefield because you want to be right and they just want to stay crazy. The fight isn't worth it because in doing so you hand over your control, your personal power. You *can* fight to "win" that. I hereby give you permission to fight *that* battle. They can "win" their self-consuming battle. You must, however, give up the urge to *fix* them. Only they can do that for themselves.

You can *influence* people who are acting crazy. How you behave can balance others when they are in a more extreme state. Imagine being in a public place and encountering a screaming lunatic. You could choose to raise your own anxiety in response and fight them on their own turf. Or, you could go in the opposite direction and hold a different internal space. Embody calm. Refuse to give up your personal power to their hysteria. Take that stance with crazy people and you won't get sucked into their crazy gravy.

You want me to get specific, do you? Okay. Let me offer a personal example. I had a client whose ex-husband brought a whole new definition of "crazy" to the table. He had been arrested for his violent temper against his ex-wife in the past. He was such a rage-aholic that he was terminated from his job for spewing his venom, especially about his ex-wife, at work. His co-workers were afraid of his temper and how quickly he went from lunacy to charm, creating a façade for management that was disturbing. Soon enough, his employers caught on. Before they fired him, they notified his ex-wife, out of fear for her safety. That night, after a proactive visit to her police department, she went home and did something pretty great. She set five audacious goals to complete in the next three months and sent the list of goals to her accountability team. Then, she loaned a friend in need a big chunk of money before she was even asked to do so.

What makes her actions so special? She could have crawled under a rock. She could have been trying to figure out how to calm him or settle him down. She could have gone insane in her head, trying to figure out his next move and stay one step ahead of him. Instead, she focused on strengthening herself and putting more of her positive energy into the world. She stayed on her battlefield and let him stay on his. Do I have to say it again? You can't fix crazy. The good news is that now that you know this, you can stop trying.

~ Changing Thoughts ~

"Great things are done by a series of
small things brought together." ~ Vincent Van Gogh

February of 2013 through all of 2014 was one of the most difficult stretches in my life. I lost both of my parents and one of my friends to death. I was part of a friendship drama that could be paralleled only by a bad reality show. I had several medical nightmares including losing my sight in one eye, dislocating my shoulder, and a host of other things. In evaluating my performance in 2014, I initially got frustrated with myself over gaining weight, falling terribly out of shape, and not meeting some of my goals, which in an "average" year would have been a cake walk for me.

Since I do what I do for a living (coach people out of their stuck states), I took a step back from this critic-fest. I started thinking about what I *did* accomplish. I wrote two books. I took my kids on a two-week cross-country road trip extravaganza, landed new clients, started a workshop series, and conducted a number of workshops. I coined these my "two lists:" *What I faced* versus *what I produced.* After reviewing that, I shared it with my community of friends and colleagues and let myself off of the hook. Everyone has two lists. You have two lists. When you want to shift your thinking, write your lists. Soak in the second list. Really let it soak in. It's not just about what you accomplished; it's about what you accomplished when you had the other list of adversity working against you. Pretty great, right?

~ Gift or Burden? ~

Gifts are often disguised as burdens. These burdens can offer a turning point in our lives. Usually we cannot see the gifts right away. There's a saying a friend of mine shared with me as she was going through her own change story: Days do not show what the years do tell. Think about that for a minute. When you look back on an experience years from now you'll have clarity you don't yet have.

What implications does this have to changing your thoughts? The magic is in the realization that you can't know now what sense you'll make of all of what happened someday so you can let go of the control over that meaning-making process. In addition, you can lean into the fear of what's happening, knowing that it'll be okay in the end. As my grandmother used to say, "things come to pass, not to stay." Let them pass. In the meantime, yell, "Is *that* all you've got? Bring it!"

~ Check Your Intentions at the Door ~

"You become what you think about." ~ Napoleon Hill

So much conflict could be eliminated if people did a better job of checking their intentions before they acted. Your intentions are thoughts you hold about what you want from any action or interaction. What are you looking to get from xyz? To build relationships or to be right? Check your intentions and be accountable for them. Don't play innocent when you're anything but. This requires that you bring your subconscious into the conscious realm. Most of what we do we do with the subconscious mind. And many of those patterns don't work for us.

When we are conscious of our role in conflict we have the power to manage it more effectively. The best way to manage it is to unplug from it. In order for a conflict to have power, it needs a complete circuit. If you detach emotionally from the conflict by keeping your intention clear from beginning to end (you might have to repeat it to yourself over and over again in your head, trust me), you don't complete the circuit.

If you find yourself in conflicts over and over again (even with the same person), ask questions instead of making statements. Set your assumptions aside and be curious instead. The results will be transformational, I promise.

If someone is bullying you or being cruel to you, that's a window to their soul, not a mirror to yours. Unless you tolerate it. Then it's about you. As I say, you can't be involved in a tug-of-war if you aren't holding the other end of the rope. Want less drama and useless conflict? Drop the rope.

~ *The Art of Setting Intentions* ~

"You gotta look for the good in the bad,
the happy in the sad,the gain in your pain,
and what makes you grateful not hateful." ~ Karen Salmansohn

When people seek my help in getting a handle on things in their professional or personal lives, the first place we start is with intentions. If you are unclear as to what you want from a situation, it's a crapshoot as to whether or not you'll end up with that result. On the other hand, if you get crystal clear on what your desired experiences and outcomes are, you are far more likely to succeed. Why? Because when you're clear on what you want, you tend to take the actions necessary to get it. It's not as simple as that since there are a host of things that distract you from getting what you want: Limited willpower, actions of others, and your belief in yourself are just a few examples.

What do you need to know about setting intentions to make you the intentions MASTER? Here are a few suggestions that I've found personally (and experienced professionally) to work wonders. Ensure that they are:

- Clear and concise, using as few words as necessary.
- Stated in positive terms ("I will be calm" vs. "I won't freak out").

- Focused on what *you* can influence or control ("I will be energetic and positive" vs. "People will be supportive and kind to me").
- Using energy that is oriented toward building, supporting, and strengthening things and others.

I think it goes without saying that the best outcomes in any change process arise from internal sources (self-motivated) and with positive thinking (I think I can vs. I should or else) instead of coming from guilt or fear (externally-based). Setting intentions is a practice based in the first step of change: The thought level. When you focus on shifting your intentions, and your thoughts that give rise to your expectations for each experience, you begin a fundamental change in the way that you see the world and yourself. Since feelings flow from thoughts, focusing on a shift in your thoughts will set the wheels in motion for a change in your feelings.

Bandura (1986) studied self-efficacy, the level of confidence that you have that you have the ability to change and master challenge. People with high degrees of self-efficacy believe that they can act upon the world and the world will respond to them in kind; that they have an effect on the outcomes in their own life. Setting intentions is a beautiful thing in this self-efficacy journey because as you set them and experience success in creating desired experiences, you come to see your own influence and entertain your vast potential.

Imagine going for a sailing trip off the coast of some tropical place. You're enjoying the expansive view of the water all around you, the warmth of the sun gazing down upon you, the light wind setting your sails in motion. In a flash, your mind is called to footage of one of those terrifying shark shows you saw on cable a few months back. All of a sudden, your every thought surrounds what will happen when a great white shark comes over the bow, snapping you up in its jaws. What's going on with your heartrate? Beating a little fast, eh? Palms getting a bit sweaty? Your blood pressure is sailing through the scale, putting you at risk for a cardiac episode (or at least a panic attack) any minute now. You are terrified, anxious, and probably near paranoid. You're beating yourself up mentally trying to figure out what on Earth made you think you should sail out here into a shark-infested feeding ground only to become lunch? If you're able to move at all, you're pacing the boat trying to figure out what your plan of escape is and how to get back to shore as soon as humanly possible. If you have one handy, you may have grabbed a pen and paper to jot down your last will and testament so your heirs can be properly compensated after your tragic passing.

Aside from having a wild imagination that I enjoy sharing with others from time to time, why did I tell you my little ditty about a shark attack? To illustrate how thoughts ("Omg, a shark is going to eat me alive") turn into feelings (panic, fear, sadness, regret) and manifest themselves in behavior (paralysis, pacing, writing a will). At any point in this path you can change the next.

If you're stuck in a pattern of thought-feeling-behavior that seems so second-nature that you don't even *realize* you're in charge of any of it, this is the key to getting unstuck. You can intervene at the thought level ("Really? A shark over the bow? Is this boat leaking blood? I should be okay."), feeling level ("It won't help to panic; if I stay calm I'll have the best chance at making the right decision about what to do next, knowing that a shark over the bow is highly unlikely"), or the behavior level ("Instead of lying here, waiting for my eventual doom, maybe I should write a list of things that usually happen to people on boats in these waters, none of which include a serpent of the deep type shark attack").

I've worked with some heavy hitters over the years and one of the rituals that the best among them have employed is something I call "Stronger Day." It works when applied to any or all aspects of your life whether it's your marriage, work, health, and so on. What's the best part about it? It's incredibly simple and intuitive because it's centered on one question: What can I do to strengthen myself today? Maybe it's a relationship you want to be better? Replace the word "myself" with "us." Say that to yourself. Say it again. Take a slow, deep breath and pause on the power of that question. It opens the door to your personal power, influence, competence, and potential. It centers you on your intention, on your true North, to be a stronger, better person, so you can focus on building. As you know, when you fail to focus, things naturally decay, like a muscle atrophying. You must strengthen what you seek to sustain or you will surely lose part or all of it.

Are you in the habit of setting intentions? Do you do it regularly or haphazardly? Do you do it only when it's an emotionally-charged situation or maybe when it's easy to be prayerful? Commit to doing it on a regular basis and watch your mind – and your life – be transformed.

~ Building Trust with Number One First ~

You have to trust yourself in order for others to trust you and for you to trust others. How do you do that? Do you what say and say what you do. It's really just as simple as that. If you make yourself a promise, keep it. If you make others a promise, keep that, too. If you are "always" late and you tell yourself that repeatedly, rest assured that you will be late, always. If you are mean to yourself, expect that you will stumble and fall in direct proportion. Treat yourself well and others are likely to do the same. The good news: If you're treating yourself well and others don't do the same, at least you're still being nice to you. It's work time.

When have you let yourself down? When have you broken your word to yourself, even if you did it in silence. Maybe you vowed to do better in some way and didn't even leave skid marks as you plowed into that same, old wall.

Stuck U.

List at least three times/situations that you let yourself down.

1.

2.

3.

What can you do to rebuild trust with yourself? List at least three things (hint: I listed out some examples in the paragraph above).

1.

2.

3.

"You don't have to control your thoughts; you just have to stop letting them control you." ~ Dan Millman

I ran across that quote in the midst of writing this book and it just encapsulates the message in this section. We have thoughts. We are not our thoughts. They come and they go. They can be fleeting or repetitive. Harmful or helpful. Yet, they are just thoughts. In the words of one of my favorite inspirational people, Mike Dooley, "thoughts become things™." I agree, but only on the premise that we let them. There's no magic spell that we cast over our thoughts to make them into something real. It's only in supporting them with attention, and pairing them with feelings and behaviors, that thoughts actually become things. Hold your thoughts wisely and your life will flourish accordingly.

As we've discussed, there are things you can control and there are things you can influence, and then there are things that are neither in your control nor under your influence. Getting those things straight in your head, in and of itself, will bring about monumental change. Consider all of the time and psychic energy you'll save if you focus your energy on what you can control and what you can influence.

What can you control? Your thoughts, feelings, and behaviors. What can you influence? Other people's thoughts, feelings, and behaviors. The rest of what goes on out there, well, that's not anything to concern yourself with if you want to stay sane and build peace in your life. Collectively, these comprise your control buckets (remember those?). This chapter is all about taking action on making a change in your life so it's seriously important that you harness your energy to take the right actions, starting with shifting your thoughts.

~ Privilege & Attitude ~

"Gratitude is not only the greatest of all virtues,
but the parent of all others." ~ Cicero

When we have privilege, we have responsibility. With luxury comes obligation. It's like women's suffrage: They paid the price, leaving us with a duty to vote. We have the luxury to live a life out loud, therefore we MUST. With opportunity comes responsibility. Otherwise it's an offensive waste.

I'm going out on a provocative limb here. We are all privileged. This isn't meant to be a political position. It's a human one. If you are on this planet and you're breathing and above ground, you have some blessings. If you have more than that going for you, you've got a host of blessings. Since you're reading this book, you've got some resources, education, and most likely a great number of things that qualify you as privileged. I'm not talking white gloves, Ivy League, mansion on the hill privileged. I'm simply referring to having most of your needs fed and wants satisfied, at least periodically.

One of my clients, a really sassy woman, was complaining about feeling a lack of energy and excitement in her life and then stopped herself and said, "Boohoo, the white girl with a loving family and a flushing toilet and guaranteed daily meals feels dispassionate." Personally, I think feeling dispassionate is a pretty big deal no matter what your circumstances are, but her quote was classic. She was forgetting to come from a place of gratitude before lamenting about what wasn't going well. The opportunity that was staring her straight in the face was to use that same gratitude foundation to build some passion for whatever she had in her life. She has *life*. When did that stop being enough?

~ Happy: The True Superpower ~

"Be happy for no reason, like a child.
If you are happy for a reason, you're in trouble
because that reason can be taken from you." ~ Deepak Chopra

There is such abundant power in happy. Starting with happy helps everything else to follow. It's energizing. It removes the rollercoaster existence of tying our happiness to a certain outcome or circumstance. Starting with happy doesn't mean that you don't feel sadness (or other negative emotions). It simply means that you approach life day-to-day with joy and recognition of your abundance.

One way to start with happy is to practice gratitude. This could be a gratitude jar: Every time you think of something to be grateful for throughout the day, no matter how small, you write it down and put it in the jar. What's great about a gratitude jar is that when you're having a crappy day you can use it like a "happiness piggy bank" and draw from it to remind yourself that things weren't always this ugly and there *are* good things out there beyond the fog. You get more of what you focus on so guard your focus with diligence. If you're constantly thinking about bad things, what are the chances that you will notice *more* bad things? Do you think you might "forget" to notice the good things? Forming an attitude of gratitude is a powerful shift that is sure to gnaw at the chains that are holding you down.

Alternatively (or additionally), you can speak your expressions of gratitude. You can engage a friend or romantic partner in a daily discussion about what you are grateful for. This might take the form of questions like, "What was the best part of your day today?", or "What is one thing that made you feel really happy today?" This kind of discussion not only helps to increase your own awareness of all that you have to be grateful for, but can also promote positive connection and experiences in your relationship with whomever you choose to have these exchanges. For example, instead of having dinner with a friend or partner and talking about all the stressors of your day, this kind of discussion leads you both to focus on the positive things, which in turn helps the stressors feel less significant, and helps you feel happier when around your friend or partner. Basically, gratitude promotes gratitude.

If you find that you're very busy and unable to stick to a regular gratitude practice, see if you can train yourself to notice things, in the moment, that you are thankful for. They can be small things. Maybe you notice that your bed is very comfortable, that your lunch is tasty, that a good friend said something nice to you, etc. It is easy to take these kinds of experiences for granted and not direct our conscious awareness to them. But training yourself to notice these kinds of things and *really* feel grateful for them can help increase your own experience of happiness.

For those of you who have watched the popular movie "The Secret" ™, you are aware of the Law of Attraction™ that was portrayed and has been written about prolifically. The Law of Attraction™ states that whatever you think about or talk about will be drawn into your life. If this is true, thinking about what you are grateful for will draw more of that to you. It seems like that's worth a try!

Have you ever played the license plate game while you were on a road trip? It's a game where you try to find a license plate from every state before the end of the trip. This game requires laser focus when you're on a road with lots of cars that are changing lanes and sporting vanity plates that make it harder to see what state they're from. What *aren't* you noticing when you're playing this game like a license plate ninja? You've probably lost some track of time, the exits you've passed, etc. The same thing happens when we are cruising through life: We focus on certain things and let other things pass us by. If we are focused on abundance and peace we will find more occasions of it. We will notice less of the other stuff. The reverse holds true, as well, so guard your focus. It is a powerful tool and you own it. *Own* it.

You might be asking yourself how this all works? There is a complex relationship between thoughts, moods, brain chemistry, and all of the systems in our bodies. Our thoughts really do trigger physiological changes in our body that affect our emotional and physical health. Basically, what you think affects how you feel (both emotionally and physically). So, if you increase your positive thoughts, like gratitude, you can increase your subjective sense of well-being as well as, perhaps, objective measures of physical health (like fewer symptoms of illness and increased immune functioning).

~ Changing Mental Models ~

"Dear Optimist, Pessimist, and Realist:
While you guys were busy arguing about the water, I drank it."
Sincerely, the Opportunist

If you change your mind, you change your experience. It's that cause and effect, believe it or not. Making something a habit: Choose to make today different. Those 12-Steppers have it right: One day at a time. You built this model of yourself over time…you can shift to a new space over time, too. Focus on today. Not on how hard tomorrow will be. You can't live tomorrow today. And you can't live yesterday over. Put your head where your feet are: Firmly planted in today.

~ Confidence & Clear Purpose ~

Confidence comes from clarity of purpose. If you're distracted and looking at a hundred things on your to-do list you won't be IN the moment you're in with full passion and intention. Without that focus, you won't be able to exude confidence. People want to work with confident, passionate people. I don't want someone who is insecure responsible for anything in my life. Because, chances are, I'll believe that even without any experience, I could do it myself with similar results.

Take financial advisors: Who would trust their money with someone who wasn't confident? Over the years, I've coached a large number of financial advisors and the most successful ones said something like this to their prospective clients: "I'm the best person for you, but make your own decision." Most of those clients choose him.

Why? Because it fits their mental model for success. He exuded confidence which leads us to believe that success will follow. For those who didn't choose him, that's self-selection, my friends. Keep on walking because you don't want those people doing business with you anyway. They will be a drain.

Making the shift from insecurity to confidence comes right down to changing your mental model from one of planning for success but expecting failure, to planning for and expecting success.

I have had countless clients who said something like, "I did everything I was supposed to do but it still failed. See? I knew it." Well, maybe you didn't do the things you were supposed to do because your focus was on failure. You had blinders on to the opportunities for success.

When you start going down that path, STOP. Ask yourself the following questions:

When has this *worked* before? When have I been successful?

What characterized that success? What did I do to make good things happen?

What created my confidence and my sense that it was going to succeed? Cheerleaders? Validation? Connection? Things in my control? A deep-rooted passion?

How can I add those positive influences to this process?

What would you do if you knew you couldn't fail? Even if you have zero confidence in yourself today, fake it, and in six months you'll have brought the success to yourself that will equal the confidence you show. Have you ever heard the phrase, "water rises to meet its own level?" You can set your sights at eye level but that will just produce more of the same of what you've already had. Set your sights high. High enough to motivate you to do more and be more than you've settled for in the past.

You do not have an infinite amount of time in your lifespan. Tomorrow is guaranteed to no one. When you give a little smidge of yourself, your true essence, to the world it's like using a sprinkler to water the planting bed: It gets the job done but it takes a while. If you only have a few minutes, you're much better off using a hose. The same goes for using your gifts in this world. Tossing some water droplets here and there just isn't effective when you've got such a short time to saturate your corner of the world. Open it up and let the world soak in the greatness that only you can offer in only the *way* that you can offer it.

~ Visioning Your Values ~

There is a common coaching activity that has become fairly common in popular culture: Making a Vision Board. It's a board that you decorate with photos or drawings or words that represent what you want in your life; the goals you have. I love the idea and have used it in my practice many times. If you haven't already created one, I highly recommend it.

Now, I want to offer up a subtle adaptation: Value Board. It's similar in its construction (using photos, drawings, and words on a board). Instead of posting images of what you *want*, you do the same for what you *value*. On this board (I used a postcard that I kept in my planner) you should represent your answers to the following questions:

What are you focused on?

What are your priorities?

What is at the center of your life?

Pick about three to five things, using words or pictures to represent them. Look at this collage each day, multiple times a day. When you get asked or invited or requested to do something that isn't contributing to one of those 3-5 things, write it down in your "parking lot" list. When you make an intentional decision to set aside one of those 3-5 things because you're in good standing with them, then and only then can you attend to something on that "parking lot" list. You'll watch the parking lot list get shorter and shorter because you won't want to let superfluous things get on it in the first place. Spend your money and time on the things on your Value Board and watch your life shift for the better.

~ My Personal Shift ~

"Things turn out best for the people who
make the best of the way things turn out." ~ John Wooden

A good friend of mine, one who met me in adulthood, asked me a powerful question after we'd known each other for years: How did you overcome your past? I paused on this question for a few minutes because I knew that what he was really asking was how I changed course from being a victim to a thriver. How did I answer him? I told him that I didn't overcome it, I integrated it. I used it as fuel to be better and stronger and not let them victimize me twice: Once when the act or acts were committed, and once again for the rest of my life. When I let those experiences drag me down I got mad at myself that I was responsible for re-vicitimizing myself every minute I let them take from my present and my future when they had already taken my past.

I put my faith in a future different than my past. I looked for every positive moment I could. I narrated my life differently. I repeated the mantra, "the only way out is through." And "God only gives you what you can handle." And "God gives his most to his best players." The being IN the Hell was in many ways not as difficult as letting it go and moving forward to a new reality. The devil you know is better than the devil you don't.

Change was frightening. I was honestly terrified of letting go of the thought structures that I held near and dear, even if they were responsible for me being a miserable, frightened, erratic, self-loathing mess. Those thought structures were *safe*. I knew what to expect. I'd proved them to be right about the world, hadn't I?

As I now tell my daughters when they tell me some negative version of a challenge they are facing, "if you believe that to be true then I have no doubt you'll prove yourself to be right." There is evidence abound to keep us exactly where we've led ourselves. If you believe that the world is a bad place you'll find plenty of evidence to make your case. If you believe that people are no good and cannot be trusted, you'll find exactly what you're looking for. If you contend that you're destined for failure, bad luck, or raw deals, sure as the sun casts its light on the Earth, you'll be right.

~ Success Stories ~

I'm going to share two of my favorite stories of corporate-level shift because I can't pick just one. I'll then share a story of a personal coaching client of mine that makes me smile just to consider it. Ready?

~ *To Win You Have to Lose* ~

During the financial services industry mayhem a number of years ago, I consulted with one of those giants that was literally hemorrhaging. Public sentiment was plummeting, as was their stock price. Customers were fleeing, wanting to get as far from that train wreck as possible. A team of us were brought in to figure out how to keep the company afloat. It was my job to train their customer service and sales team on dealing with their client base, trying to save every customer relationship possible. When we came in, they had been trained on how to "win" the conversation with these agitated and frightened clients by towing the party line, telling each customer the "facts" about the company's solvency. Sounds reasonable, right? We've been trained to "win" and "convince" so this approach fits and should work, right? Wrong. It wasn't working.

We got in there and turned their approach on its head. We taught their personnel to start by agreeing with the customers, showing the utmost empathy and understanding for their fear and lack of trust. Yup. We sure did. What were we thinking? We knew that people like to be understood and respected and right. When the company's personnel told the customers they were wrong by throwing "facts" at them, the customers trusted the company *less*. I don't know about you, but I wouldn't leave my money with a company I didn't trust. They had to rethink their purpose on each call to be to build trust. Then and only then could they hope to bring the caller to their line of thinking and have a productive conversation about those "facts."

I'll bet that you want to know what happened to the company? Its stock rebounded and it continues to prosper today.

~ Sinking Ship ~

Every company has a story about a project or program that went off the rails. The less fortunate organizations have had that program almost take the company down with it. I was consulting for one of these companies and was brought in at the executive level to facilitate a meeting to get to the bottom of the crisis and navigate their way back out. Sounded easy enough (sarcasm). In planning for this meeting, which was to include the heavy hitters from each of the involved sectors, I was (jokingly) told to wear a flak jacket and brush up on my jujitsu. This meeting was not for the faint of heart, but if you haven't guessed it yet, there isn't a challenge I've shrunk from.

So, in I went, ready for anything and everything. I set strict boundaries for the meeting, mandating that no one (not even the Board members in attendance) could speak to anyone who was not in the meeting for the **entire day**. I was clear that they had been using the system against itself, doing the "it's ***their*** problem" routine until they were in their current crisis state. I was having none of that. Change was not going to occur until they started to see that each and every one of them was part of the problem and could therefore be part of the solution. I wrote the name of their company on a huge sheet of paper that I placed on the floor in the space between us. Every time any one of them started to point fingers of blame at another person or department, I halted them and pointed to the paper on the floor. I kept asking, "Does this serve the interest of the name on this sheet?" It was a long day, but a highly productive one. New alliances were created. A plan was drafted. The group walked out of there with a mission: To save their company by focusing on helping, not blaming, one another.

Within a year, that program was boasting a 60% sales increase. It went from being the reason that the company might go under to one of the reasons it was profitable. All it took was a thought shift to start that beautiful cascade of events.

~ *Secret Language* ~

My first book spurred me to start a monthly women's group to discuss its content and lessons, encouraging attendees to find their voice and live a more authentic and joyful life. One of the attendees was every facilitator's dream: She soaked up the lessons like a sponge, asking challenging questions so she could really put the lessons to use in her life.

One night, she reported that she and her husband had been having troubles as it related to disciplining the kids. Her husband was always on the road for business, so most of that activity fell to her. When he returned, they struggled to find a rhythm, usually tripping over one another as they both tried to manage the kids simultaneously. After consulting with me on the issue and discussing "control buckets" she raced home to share this concept with her husband. She described how their "tripping over one another" was really about confusing who was in control of what at any given time, not that either one of them was *wrong.*

The very next morning, the kids were doing what kids do and she and her husband fell into their old "tripping" pattern. Very quickly, she used a charades-type symbol to refer to her "control bucket." He nodded and stopped dead in his tracks. The rest of the morning was as smooth as silk. Later that morning, he texted her and thanked her for making that sign and they agreed that this was their new way of communicating that so they didn't have to publicly discuss their struggle in front of the kids (a trigger for him).

Ahhh…yet another success story and all it took was a little perspective shift, a little distance from the emotion and personalization of an issue, and some private codes. Change is good.

What made all of these stories successful? These individuals, departments, and companies started to think about themselves, one another, and their conflicts differently so that they could make different decisions about their behavior. Subtle but powerful language shifts became part of the cultural (and familial) conversation. The other thing they all had in common was that they employed the use of a "third eye" to help them see where their thinking was limiting their potential.

~ The "Big Or" ~

"I am not a product of my circumstances.
I am a product of my decisions." ~ Stephen Covey

We get really invested in seeing things the way that we see them. There's a line from a movie or television show from way back (I don't recall the source) where one of the characters says, "don't confuse me with the facts." Many of us operate on this premise every day, assuming we are right about something just because we think of it a certain way. Just because we think of it one way doesn't make it so. Before you get all offended and haughty, accusing me of assuming that you don't know what you're talking about, please hear me out.

The "Big Or" approach doesn't mean that you are wrong for assuming whatever it is that you're assuming. It simply invites you to follow your pronouncement with, "OR…" In effect, what you're saying is that your assumption is simply *one* way of looking at things. To adopt this method properly and enjoy yourself in the process, you really have to accentuate the "or," very dramatically. The correct spelling of the word the way it should sound in your mind is "orrrrrrrrrrrrr" (add more r's as you see fit). This approach opens up possibilities and can shift perceptions without a crazy amount of work.

Once you've let your mind say "orrrrrr," start brainstorming what else could possibly be going on? If a clerk is rude to you, you might assume that they are a jerk who is in the wrong job. Orrrrrr, maybe their boss just let them know that they are now scheduled to work a double shift because someone called in sick and they have two young children at home, one who is sick, and the kids have been texting them non-stop for the past hour begging her to come home. Still mad at her? Sure, her behavior isn't great and you might not recommend her for employee of the month, but are you harboring disgust and frustration at her anymore? Have those emotions been replaced with a smidge of compassion? Just a smidge?

All it took was a two-letter (well, seven-letter the way I've spelled it) word to start world peace. Pretty incredible, huh? If nothing else, the negative effect of her attitude on your day has been lessened. This technique works like a charm with people we know better (colleagues, customers, friends, family members) because we might actually *know* what the "or" is. We might know that it's review time and their meeting with the boss is coming up in a few hours so if they are snappy with us, we can assume that they are ticked at us "orrrrrr" they are nervous as heck that they are going to miss out on a raise. Feeling a little less reactive?

The magic of the "Big Or" rests in claiming your personal power, getting unstuck from the pattern of assumptive behavior that's had you in its grasp for years, and being more peaceful in your relationships with others, regardless of their behavior. What does this have to do with personal power? Personal power is about calm and influence. You have a much harder time remaining calm when you are reacting to people and their ever-changing moods. You possess far more influence when you can be intentional, as well as calm, in interacting with others. There's a reason that squirrels don't rule the jungle and lions do. Calm power.

~ Shift the Narrative ~

"People are disturbed not by things,
but by the view which they take of them." ~ Epicetus

The human brain is a powerful thing. It's responsible for our life itself, and for our experience of it. How we think about things drives how we feel about them and what we do in response to them. Without thought, we are nothing. In those thoughts, we build our future on the foundation we've crafted in the past. How we think about our past creates our understanding of the present and our views of the future. You're not only the star on the stage that is your life, you're also the narrator. You guide the message you share with yourself and others that shapes your expectations of yourself and the world around you.

Do you have a narrative of your past that isn't working well for you? Write your "old narrative" down on paper. Spend a good 15-30 minutes writing every lousy thing you've been reliving over and over again in your head (or in the words spewing out of your mouth). Once you've expelled it all onto paper, have a burning ceremony. Watch it burn. Smell the aroma. Watch it curl up. Let it go. See the ashes float into the air, appreciating that what has happened is done and you get to rewrite your story accentuating any aspect of it you want. The pen is in your hand; use it deliberately and wisely. Now, ask yourself these questions:

How can I see the same experiences differently?

Was there anything good that happened while the bad things were happening?

What good *wouldn't* have happened if the bad things hadn't happened?

Who wouldn't you have met?

What challenges wouldn't you have been able to boast about overcoming?

How would you be different today if you hadn't had those challenges?

I clearly haven't offered enough space in this book for you to write this all out, so grab a journal and start writing. Don't stop until you've got mostly positive words and happy memories. You can use humor to lighten even the worst things. Use humor. Resist sarcasm when you can because sarcasm houses anger and that's not going to serve you in letting go of the negative hold your past has had on you.

You've got a new past narrative. Now what? What can you do today to make tomorrow different? It's all in those pesky things called "words." The way we speak about things directly affects how we feel and behave. Change the words, change your life. How can you figure out what you are doing that is harming your present and limiting your future? Here are some questions to ask yourself to see where you might want to take some action:

- Do you use flexible language when you describe things? Do you avoid words like "always" and "never?" Do you use "sometimes" and "in the past" instead?
- Do you use words that are filled with possibilities and compassion or limitations and judgment?
- Do you see things in black and white, viewing only one option as "truth?" Instead, can you entertain the "Big Or?"
- Do you see things emanating from fate or from choice?
- Do you find yourself saying, "I have to do this" or do you say, "I choose to do this?"
- Do you see yourself as the hero of your own life or the victim of it? Do you see your strengths or are you focused on your weaknesses?

Now that we've got a handle on your head, it's time to move down your spine and address your other major organ: Your heart.

~ Changing Feelings ~

Thoughts lead to feelings. Sounds easy enough, right? How we think about something, how we interpret cause, intent, and meaning lead us to feel a certain way about it. If we shift the meaning-making process, acknowledge that thoughts are not anything but thoughts and they are not in charge of us, and that we can shift our thinking, we can change the way we emotionally experience ourselves, other people, and the world.

~ Power of Feelings ~

"What you want to ignite in others,
must first burn inside yourself." ~ Aurelius Augustinus

How many times have you heard someone say, "but I can't help how I feel." C'mon, be honest; you've said that a time or two (or 1,000). I contend that we most certainly *can* help how we feel. We give "feelings" too much power. They are real yet not nearly as "in control" as we mistake them to be. Our feelings are as much in our heads as our thoughts are. Why? Because feelings are based on the interpretation of our situation, how we understand our lot in life. When we truly *think* differently we *feel* differently, too. Some of you are shaking your head right now because you say, "I've tried thinking happy, positive thoughts but I still feel angry/sad/frustrated."

You're absolutely right. Yup, thinking happy thoughts if you don't believe them on any level is just ensuring that you're apt to feel even worse than you did if you didn't think those happy thoughts in the first place.

The most important relationship you'll ever have is the one you have with yourself. If you don't trust yourself you're in for a rocky road at best. When you're thinking a happy thought but at the very same time you're thinking, "This is bull," you might as well be running over your good intentions with a tractor trailer truck for all the good you're doing. In order to truly shift your feelings about something, you need to buy into the thoughts you're entertaining. Maybe not 110%, but at least in spirit. You can't be waiting to fail in shifting your thoughts and adjusting your feelings and expect to succeed.

Your natural inclination is to be right, whether being right is helpful to your overall health, functioning, and success. If you're thinking that you're a bad friend but you want to be better and you try to tell yourself that you *are* a good friend, you will undoubtedly fumble in your friendships just to prove yourself right. Being right equals being safe and in control. You've been succeeding at failure, get it? You've been right about being a bad friend, which offers some comfort. If you make attempts to be a good friend, you might fail, which is scary.

Instead, you stay wrapped up in the comfy blanket of failure and falling short, blaming yourself, others, and the world for what you don't have and who you are not. I have some news for you: You've had the power inside of you the entire time to transform anything and everything in your life.

The Holy Grail is to spend time and energy in building the relationship you have with yourself. Ever hear the reference about being your own worst enemy? Yup. Truth. The surefire way to do that is to start being honest with yourself and admit that you've been standing in your own way all of this time, and understandably so, because the magnetism of safety is strong.

It's in the "understandably so" that so many people get lost. We get caught in the track of self-recrimination and don't give ourselves compassion for the lot we've sold ourselves. We are always here for a reason. Our condition (past and current) has served us somehow. If we chastise ourselves about it then our subconscious will just fight that much harder for validation.

You might not be able to hear your subconscious clearly but when you're busy beating yourself up for what you have or haven't done, here's what it's likely yelling: "Don't you <u>understand</u> me? Don't you get how hard it's been? Don't you care about my pain and struggle?"

If you did your homework and read my book, *Feed the Need*, you know that when one of your needs isn't being met you're likely to behave in destructive, dysfunctional ways. One of those needs is validation and we all have it no matter how self-sufficient we are. If you refuse to validate yourself, that part of you will find a way, like a flower finds sunlight, to be heard. Being heard usually means acting out in order to prove that little voice right about you.

Is that what you want? I know you want to yell, "of course not!" but it's not that simple, as I've explained. You've been getting something out of being messed up and you have to reconcile with that truth before you can move forward.

~ Leaving the Haters Behind ~

"Those who tried to break you are expecting you to be in fight mode. Conquer them with your peace." ~ Thema Davis

When I first left my marriage, I was certain that I'd made the right decision for myself and my children, but I still held onto a healthy degree of guilt for making that choice. Over the next number of years, my ex-husband made it abundantly clear through every manner of communication that I was to blame for every ounce of disorder and pain experienced by our children, him, and me. I did my best to push those castrations aside but my subconscious had been sent that message for years so his words hit fertile ground. I felt responsible so I felt guilty so I felt I had to pay the price.

How did I accomplish that? I struggled financially. I stressed about money and did just enough professionally to not go completely under. I did the same personally, in my friendships and romantic relationships. At a very base level, I believed that if I succeeded then I was selfish and unworthy and hadn't suffered enough for my "sins."

Then one day, in celebrating my five-year anniversary flying solo, I made a pronouncement: I was done suffering. I had paid whatever karmic debt that might be floating around out there and I was "even." The most amazing thing happened: Within days of saying this out loud and shifting my thinking to allow for abundance instead of survival, I received call after call for my services, at premium prices. I made more in 19 days than I'd made the prior YEAR. Amazing, right?

Why did I tell you that story? To illustrate that no amount of "positive thinking" did me much good in that first five-year stretch. Happy thoughts alone didn't cut it. What I was missing was validating the purpose that was being served in my struggle: Assuaging guilt. Once I came to terms with the fact that guilt was driving me to <u>not</u> succeed I was able to make a different decision about it. I decided to believe that I had paid the price (if there was one to pay in the first place) and I could let that responsibility go. Are you ready to let go of that cement block that is holding you down?

You'll FEEL passion after you ACT on things with passion.

Are you afraid you won't feel anything? That if you detach, feelings will build up and you'll end up depressed or anxious. That doesn't have to happen. You are substituting one feeling (disdain/resentment) for another (passion/excitement). It's not about FEELING the passion upfront because there is an organic reason "making" you do so. Instead, it's about DECIDING to exhibit passion because it serves you (in the long run).

You *feel* how you *think*. You feel in response to your actions (how you "do"). Love is a feeling and an action. You can love (action) ugly, despicable things. That feels untruthful? Okay, I'll grant you that.

But it's temporary. You attitude and feelings shift when your "fake" attitude and behaviors shift.

Do you hate your job but for some reason you are stuck in it? You have an option other than going crazy five (or more) days out of seven. Think of your job like an arranged marriage: You can either rail against it or you can find things to love about it so that you can live each day in passion and joy. The good news for YOU is that you can get a divorce someday, without being stoned to death or having someone take your goats as penance.

~ Bless & Release ~

A cornerstone of the "bless and release" process is forgiveness. Forgiveness. I have yet to meet a person who hasn't struggled with forgiveness. When someone hurts us, it seems to be in our DNA to hold onto that like a warrior, reminding ourselves of the injury over and over again. We hear the person's name and we shudder. And wince. And growl. Yes, growl. We are mad and hurt and often we want revenge. We rejoice when they flounder. We seek out the chance to see them with their proverbial pants down. Whatever it is that the person did to you, you hold onto it with a death grip, certain that it's the right thing to do because *they hurt you.* It's the annoying need for validation rearing its ugly head.

The only problem with this approach is that it <u>ties you to</u> the very person who caused you pain. Read that again. Oh, you want to be stubborn because you think you got that and you don't need to repeat it. Too bad. This is my book. Here it is: It <u>ties you to the very person who caused you pain</u>. You're saying you can't stand them and what they did to you, but you live a certain portion of your life revolving around it, and them. Gross.

How do I know this? I've done it, trust me. Even though I'm paid to guide people through the forgiveness process, I can be a stubborn mule when I've been injured. Even more so when my kids have been hurt in the process. Mama bear comes out and I'm not letting go for anything. I want my kids' pain to stop, yet, I'm not in charge of the other person so I'm stuck controlling my end of things. I trick myself into thinking that if the other person pays for hurting my kids and me that somehow all will be right in the world. That's justice, right? Isn't that held sacred in our culture? There's some big book out there, though, that teaches that an eye for an eye leaves the whole world blind.

What's the alternative? Break the hold, the connection that the person (and their actions) has over you. Let go of the anger and resentment. Sounds easy, right? Um, no, not so much. I was burned, big time, by a woman who called me her best friend, whose kids were my kids' best friends. We were family by all accounts. I gave to her and her kids, often beyond reason. My time, resources, energy, attention, and so much more. Then something happened in our village that tore us all apart. I took the lion's share of the blame, and punishment. She didn't just walk away quietly. She stormed out of my life and stonewalled my kids and me from her and her children. There was to be no contact. No words. Nothing. Ever. No conversation about it. Can you imagine *me* not being allowed a conversation? Not able to use words to attempt to heal things? It was horrible, vicious, and punishing. It was my personal Dante's Inferno.

I spent countless hours pouring over the "why" and the injustice of it all. I received all sorts of emotional support and compassion, but she didn't budge. My family was shut out in a very sudden and very public fashion. It hurt like you can only imagine. It was bullying, plain and simple, and by someone who had "loved" me once which made it so much worse. I was devastated. I didn't want to be her friend after that, trust me. She showed her true colors and I felt blessed that I wasn't near her and her toxicity anymore. But her actions had tentacles that kept creeping into my life, and we crossed paths all the time. I braced myself emotionally every time I anticipated seeing her. It was an energy suck of tremendous magnitude.

My dear friend, Lisa, suggested that I write a letter. *To* her???! Nope. *From* her. Saying what she would say to me if she had the capacity to be authentic and clear and calm. If she could explain herself to me, with all of her warts and scars exposed for me to see. It took me over a year to finally listen to her sage advice (I told you I was stubborn!) and write the bloody letter.

An amazing thing happened as soon as I finished it. I was able to let go. I let go of the hurt and my fantasies of her suffering the way she had made me suffer. I was able to see her for the damaged and insecure person that she was, who saw no other way than to cut me off at the knees in order to protect her fragile self-image from my challenge. After I read the letter, I apologized to her (in my head, folks, please!) for my contribution to our path, releasing myself from the burden of being connected to her and our past. It was transformational. Each time I see her now I am not filled with resentment, but instead with compassion. And a healthy dose of pity.

> "Yes, forgiving others feels good. But I've always found
> that kicking them in the groin twice and
> then forgiving them feels even better." ~ Buster Guru

~ Power of a Picture ~

Unless you've been living under a rock, chances are you've heard about using visualization to manifest desired circumstances in your life. Visualization is essentially creating an image in your mind's eye of a future that you want so that you guide yourself toward that outcome. It's like being stuck in a harsh winter and imagining being on a warm, secluded beach, feeling the hot sun's rays washing over you, smelling the salt water, and hearing the crash of the waves onto the shore. You just wiped the sweat off your brow, didn't you? If you have the means, you're probably surfing the Web for travel deals to the Caribbean.

That's the essence of visualization: Building an end point in your head with enough compelling details to drive you toward it. Visualization requires that you focus on the other side, just like when you're getting onto or off of a train. You don't focus your energy and aim toward the space *between* the platform and the train. You focus on the target. Rock climbers don't attend too much on where they've been; they focus on where they're going, where they're going to hook their next clip, or they die. Plain and simple. You aren't apt to die if you don't get this visualization thing right but your dream may.

Why hasn't everyone who's heard of visualization retired in wealth to an island somewhere? First, it's not the end all be all of creating the life you've imagined. There's more to realizing your dream than simply visualizing it, but it's a critical step and it has to be done right. If you want it to be the powerful tool it can be, make sure you:

- Create your Vision Board or book that contains the photos, pictures, drawings, and words that describe what you want. Hang it prominently in a place that you see every day, preferably first thing in the morning and last thing in the evening.
- Create your Value Board with images and/or words about what your core values are and resist spending time or money on things not on the board until the things on the board are fully satisfied. Remember that what people value isn't known by what they say; it's known by what they spend their time and their money on.
- Just like a goal, describe your desired change in the highest possible detail and write your narrative down in a journal or incorporate it into your Vision Board. Tell everyone you know about it, sharing what you've described and displayed with your

"accountability group" (the team of people you can rely on to hold you accountable to your goals).

- Talk about "when" and not "if" when you share your plan with others (and when you talk to yourself about it).
- Remember that visualization means nothing without taking the necessary actions to make it a reality! If you're planning to climb all seven summits you'll need to actually get your butt off the sofa and not just watch other people doing it on the Travel Channel™.

Now that you've learned some tools you can use to create shifts in your thoughts and your feelings, it's time to address the end of the chain: Your behaviors.

~ Changing Behaviors ~

At the end of the day, your success or failure isn't dictated by your thoughts or your feelings. It's dictated by your actions. I've given you tools to modify your thoughts which then influence your feelings. I've offered tools to modify your feelings when those may be getting off track, despite your improved line of thinking. This is the step where the rubber meets the road. If you effectively manage your thoughts and feelings but then don't follow it up with a monitoring and management of your behaviors, you'll most likely give up on the process because your behaviors are what usually receive the most feedback and reward. Ready to master your actions?

~ Toolkit...Five Things That Will Get You Unstuck ~

Let's start this section off by reviewing five actions that will support your thinking and feeling shifts and solidify your changes through behavior changes.

1. **Journaling.** This practice helps you to process what's happening and offers a brain dump so you can free up some mental space for more useful things. People who journal have a greater rate and depth of recovery, visit the doctor less, and I contend that I'd find them with more Emotional Agility. Getting things out of your head and on paper allows you to review what you've been thinking and feeling. As you know from this change process, identifying what you're thinking and where it might be "off" allows you to shift your thinking and then adjust how you feel. When you feel differently, you behave differently. Want to change your path? Journal.

2. **Talking About It:** Let me be crystal clear. Talking about an issue is *not* a replacement for doing something, but it can act as a catalyst and an accountability step. Much like writing things down, talking about them makes them real. Having a goal in secret is one thing: Sharing it with the world makes it real and holds you accountable to others. Share it and you'll nail it. Telling other people what you're struggling through is a public pronouncement, as well, so there is inherent accountability, potential validation and support, and challenge. When you share your thoughts with another person (no, your dog doesn't count), you can welcome in new perspectives and suggestions on how to shift your thinking. One important point: Don't just share things with a person who is your mental twin, who thinks about things the same way that you do. Clearly, this might serve to validate you but it won't challenge your assumptions. If you're in it to win it in the change department, branch out and share your struggle with someone who might (gasp!) disagree with you.

3. **Just Do It:** I've coached countless people over the years and the vast proportion of them dealt with anxiety about making a move in the right direction. They got stuck because they stopped moving. Get it? It's only possible to get stuck if you're not in motion. Put yourself in motion. When in doubt, act. I mean that literally. Take one small step toward the change you want by

pretending that you're just playing a role, acting a part. If your mind is your enemy, make your body your friend. If you don't "feel" like going to the gym, go. Your mind will catch up. This is one way in which the thoughts-feelings-behaviors chain doesn't necessarily apply. If your thoughts and feelings are getting in your way and you're stuck, move first. Move a little, move a lot. Just *move.*

4. **Get a Partner:** Misery loves company and so does change. When you want to get in shape, get a workout buddy who keeps you honest. Group weight loss systems are popular for the same reason. Have a change you want to tackle? Find a friend or co-worker who is up for their own challenge (doesn't have to be the same trait or behavior, and it often works better if they are different) and form an accountability team. Check in daily or weekly, depending on the change. Celebrate your strides, nudge each other along during your slips. Build a network of friends, family, colleagues, and contacts to call upon for when you need this sort of partnership. Nothing knocks you off balance like thinking or feeling like you're all alone, a one-man/woman show.

5. **Establish a Reward System:** You can combine this one with some of the other tactics on this list. Admit it, you're like a dog. Yes, you. You want to get a cookie when you've done something well. Use your natural drive for validation by setting up rewards ("cooooooookies") when you practice certain skills or reach certain milestones. Maybe it's a present to yourself of material goods, a treat, or time off/away. If you're the employer, remember that we all have a need for acknowledgment and appreciation. To be caught doing something right. Sometimes we get so caught up in correcting and "guiding" that we forget how important it is to tell someone that we see the good they did. To throw them a cookie. Just a cookie. Not a platter, especially if they are screwing up more than they are succeeding. But a cookie. Just to give them a taste of the reward that we all hunger for. You'll

soon find that they feel encouraged to be better so they can "earn" more.

As you can see, modifying your behavior is not nearly as complicated as modifying your thoughts and feelings. Sometimes making a change to how you act is just that, an act. Fake it till you make it, as my aunt always tells me. Along the way to making it, you'll start believing that the faking it isn't so fake after all. Now that we've covered some no-brainers for changing your behaviors, it's time to dig deeper and fill up your backpack of options to get the change you desire.

"The secret of change is to focus all of your energy, not on fighting the old, but on building the new." ~ Socrates

~ Breaking Free From Calcification ~

"It's hard to beat a person who never gives up." ~ Babe Ruth

The longer you stay stuck, the harder it is to break free. If you've been behaving badly, the longer you hold your position, the more damage you'll do. If and when you decide to behave better, you'll have a lot of work to do. You'll have to admit your role and responsibility over the longer haul. And make amends. And heal relationships that may be forever compromised. Your actions may be unforgivable to the people who you injured or alienated. Trust may be forever broken. Cement sets quickly. Seeing things in only one way holds you in the cement, waiting for it to dry. We often create cement to make things look black and white. We want to be right, not wrong. We want to be blameless. We set up "us vs. them" dynamics. In sports, in politics, companies, and in life.

We can all call to mind a person in our present or past who seemed to have every reason in the world to stop a certain behavior or habit but never did. They were faced with losing everything that meant anything to them, or just living a miserable existence, and it didn't matter. They stayed stuck. People spent countless hours trying to convince them of the error of their ways, enlightening them with what they "should" do, to no avail.

These individuals were not stupid, or insane. (Well, some were one or both, especially if their behavior rose to the level of narcissism, for instance.) Why did they refuse to change, even when it seemed to be in their best interest and it made complete sense to do so? Calcification, that's why. When we convince ourselves that we are "right" and everyone who disagrees with us is "wrong," we hold onto our position with formidable vigor. The more public the battle, the more extreme and firmly held the position. Once our ego is invested in being right (and the other person "wrong"), it is difficult to consider other viewpoints and to admit that we may be wrong. That we may have done injury to others by acting in accordance with our position. As we fully recognize the carnage we have left in our wake, it is often easier to remain convinced of our infallibility than to risk being wrong and have to make amends for our actions. No one likes egg on their face, and the drier it is, the harder it is to get it off.

Imagine you're standing on stage taking part of a game show predicament of choosing which door to open, in hopes of winning the best possible prize package. But in this case, you could see that one door opened to a protracted process of admitting you were wrong for years, reconciliation, seeking forgiveness, earning back trust, and mending relationships that had been strained or abolished by your behavior and your certainty that you were right. The other door opened up to your same, consistent reality, where you believed in what you were doing was right and just. And behind that door might be the same old, same old, but it was comforting in that it was unchanged. Without challenge. You can see why you might just want to stay right where you are.

Please don't. It's a miserable life. Change is hard, I know. But, it's worth it.

~ Using Stop, Center, Move ~

In the "thoughts" section of this chapter, we discussed setting intentions and the power of that practice in creating the life we want. In order to get the best out of setting intentions, use the "Stop, Center, Move" strategy. How does it work? When we are caught up in running from moment to moment, we are reactive. We walk (or run) into situations without a thought or plan so we play the behavioral equivalent of ping pong. Someone says or does something that upsets us and we respond in kind. We leave the meeting and text or email our friend or spouse, bitching about the latest drama and scoping out a game plan for revenge or evening the scales.

Want a different reality? The power is truly yours. Before you head into your next meeting, stop and consider what you want from that meeting. Is it consensus? Understanding? Productivity? Clarification? Center on that intention, whatever it is. Take a deep breath or two, knowing that if you align your thoughts (what you want, your intention) with your feelings (the emotions you indulge when things start happening) and your behaviors (how you respond to what's going on around you), the outcome is bound to be the best it can possibly be. Once you've stopped and centered on your intention, then, and only then, can you move (go to that next situation).

A very intelligent and accomplished client of mine, for whom I hold a great deal of respect, called me one day and told me, "your Stop, Center, Move approach crashed and burned. I lost my temper in that meeting, just like I feared I would." I hate to fail. I really do. For a moment, I feared that I had failed my client by advising that he use a technique that wasn't effective.

As I probed a bit, I found that he had missed the critical step in this practice: He moved in a direction that was inconsistent with his intention. He went into the meeting knowing that no one was prepared yet he had the intention of "resolution." He was *bound* to be disappointed and frustrated. Like most of us, when he gets disappointed and frustrated, he gets irritable and reactive. So, that's exactly what happened. When you set an intention that is completely inconsistent with the situation only a miracle could make that happen. Don't waste your time on wishing for miracles. Instead, direct your efforts at things you can control and influence. Adjust your next action, if necessary, but make darned sure that you stay firm in your intention and watch things change, slowly but surely.

Before you are set to see that person, make sure you calm yourself and practice my Stop, Center, Move technique. I've had executives swear that they don't have time to Stop, Center, Move. Want to know what I tell them? "Even E.R. surgeons stop and wash their hands. Take that 30 seconds.

~ People…And Game Changers ~

"It's better to walk alone than with a crowd
going in the wrong direction." ~ Diane Grant

Every challenge is an opportunity: My pre-teen daughter asked me the other day what the purpose of being a mom was if it wasn't a popularity contest? This was in the midst of her cajoling me and attempting to get me to let her stay home from school, indefinitely. When I said, "nope, you're going to school and are going to face up to the things you think you can't," this discussion turned to why I wasn't too concerned if she liked me or not. I told her that my job as a mom was to allow her to be challenged and to get into some hot water so that she could figure out how to get out of it on her own; that I was always there to help and to advise, but that strong and positive self-esteem wasn't going to come from me doing things *for* her. Then the hard truth emerged: I wasn't going to always be there to do things for her or to protect her from the big, bad wolves.

I knew this first-hand, and I also appreciated that I was left to my own devices far too young and far too often. My upbringing showed me that I could handle anything. No one was going to handle my business for me. I was on my own. Now, please don't get me wrong: I don't want my daughters to feel abandoned and without my love and support. But challenge forces us to figure things out, to look inside and outside for resources, and to appreciate the quieter and more abundant moments. Without challenge, we would be psychic couch potatoes. They (challenges) make up the very fabric of our lives. We come out on the other end stronger than we entered. We may be tired and disheveled, or we may find ourselves triumphant and energized by our mastery of the moment. Either way, we emerge victorious knowing that the ugly and painful moments of life do not control our inner joy or predict our path of higher purpose.

You can't change other people but you can influence them. You have more power to influence them when you are focused on changing yourself. All too often in companies, people in the organization feel powerless to do anything because "someone" has the authority over resources or processes and that "someone" isn't them.

If this is you, you feel like salmon swimming upstream with the best of intentions. You find a dam that's blocking your path. You keep ramming your little fishy head, but no dice. You can't get any further. You're driving yourself nuts. You're not receiving your just desserts, the resources you need, and those that were promised to you. It's like getting dropped behind enemy lines and you think you have a machine gun in your sack and all you have is a butter knife. What can you do?

If you're like a lot of my clients when I first find them, you do nothing. You get stuck and you resign yourself to your current reality, thinking that this is how it'll always be. I'm paid to challenge the status quo so I'll tell you what I've told them.

Think tactically. Think strategically. Stop making yourself crazy waiting for the right supplies to arrive. Make do with what you have. You're in charge of your response and your intentions. Despite what you might have been brainwashed to think, you're not in charge of the end results. Not directly. You can only influence the end results through influence and good forces conspiring for you. Your job is to manage every last thing that is in your locus of control to the best of your abilities, always looking for ways to be more influential through calm, centered personal power. That, my friends, is a game changer.

~ Page 44: It's About to Get Personal ~

Anyone who read the first edition of my book, *Feed The Need*, or watched me present on it probably remembers the infamous "page 44" (it moved to page 48 in the second edition, fyi). On the original page 44, I described an exercise (a pretty erotic one, to be honest) to build deep intimacy with your partner. A colleague urged me to always have a "page 44" in my books, to give people a tool to bring and keep more love and passion into their lives, since that's what builds meaning in our time here on Earth. As soon as I started this book, I've been on the lookout for such a lesson to share.

I was watching a very poignant love story in which the girl faces death and has a decision to make as to whether or not she wants to fight to survive. The audience is taken through her memories, building a case in both directions. Her lover comes to her side as she lies there unconscious and begs her to stay and fight. He promises his life to her, through tears of anguish. And it made me think: If they had known that their last kiss was going to be their last kiss, what would *that* kiss have felt like? If they'd known that the last time they lay together that they would never again be in one another's tender embrace? How might it have been different? For those of us who have had the rare pleasure of knowing that moment, hopefully before a break up and not before a death, it's an intense experience. Every cell in your body is alive with passion, fear, love, sorrow, and joy. You pour everything you can into it, and draw everything you can back out of it. It's unparalleled.

Now, here's a question for you: What if you kissed your lover like that every time? What if every time you lay together, you treasured it like you'd never be there again? Would you be more tender? Would you pay closer attention to every curve of their body, freckle on their face, contour of their smile? Would you be more in tune with their breath, the softness of their skin, the look in their eyes? And what if that intensity was brought to every encounter?

You're welcome.

I have a surprise for you, too. You can apply this to every interaction in your life. How? Imagine that each time you speak to someone it could be the last. How would that conversation be different? Would you be more risk-taking? More honest? Would you bring more of the real you to the table? Someone asked me once how I knew I was doing good coaching work and do you know what I told them? When I'm fighting back tears. That may sound odd, but it's completely accurate. When I am really connecting with someone and making a powerful impact on their life, it moves me deeply. That's what life is all about, after all. Connecting with other people and making a positive difference in their life. Easing suffering. Offering hope. Try it…you might like it.

~ Ping-Pong-Catch ~

When someone throws something at you, you get to decide how to react. I call it the "Ping-Pong-Catch" model. Most of us have played ping-pong or something like it. It's a fast-paced, high-intensity game designed for those who have fast reflexes. Then there's catch. A nice, relaxing game of catch. When you're playing ping-pong you are rewarded for hitting whatever comes towards you right back at your opponent, hoping to catch them off guard so they'll miss your serve or hit it out of bounds in return. It's a win-lose game. There is no award given out for "niceness" or "a gentle spirit." You are there to win. In catch, on the other hand, you need the other person to succeed *with* you or you don't succeed (or have much fun).

When someone is coming at you with hostility you have a choice: Play ping-pong or play catch. Playing ping-pong is reactive and you're likely to get in a fight. If you play catch, you get to hold and wait before you respond. The time spent waiting gives you the chance to gain perspective and make a conscious choice about how to respond. With choice there is power. I don't mean power over someone because that can be violated and it should never be your goal. I mean power over yourself. You hold more of your personal power when you practice pausing between thought and behavior. Slow down that thought-feeling-behavior chain and you will come into your maximum personal power, effectiveness, and success.

~ Concluding Thoughts ~

It's time that I tell you a secret: You can change your behavior and your results without initially changing your thoughts and feelings. All a change requires if for you to start moving. Get on the field. Experience the change. See yourself differently. Then you'll think differently. And act differently. Rise up to your expectations. It's a riskier strategy for the thinkers among us who might never make it past the threshold, but for those of you who can hack that approach, by all means, go for it! You have my blessing and my encouragement.

Key Chapter Concepts

- To have change, you have to want it.
- Big changes can, and do, come in baby steps.
- You can't fix crazy but you can stay sane with perspective.
- Changing your thoughts changes your feelings which opens up new behavior patterns, starting with setting good intentions.
- Just saying "or" transforms your life through flexible thinking.
- Use Stop, Center, Move to keep calm and focused.

"For the resolute and determined there is time and opportunity." ~ Ralph Waldo Emerson

ADJUSTMENT

"I have not failed.
I've just found 10,000 ways that won't work." ~ Thomas Edison

~ Introduction ~

Ever had major surgery? Did you go back to work the next day, jumping right back into your old routines? If you did, you're not getting any accolades from me. The body needs time to heal and adapt to the new reality. I've run into all sorts of people who have gotten knee or hip replacements and do you know what follows surgery? Physical therapy. If the reconstructive surgery is the "Action" step in the change process, physical therapy is the "Adjustment" step. You've committed action toward some changes in your life; now it's time to step back and see what you've accomplished and may need to do differently to get to your best state.

In this chapter, I'll take you through the Adjustment process so you can make sure that your change sticks. It's all about addressing corrections as you move along the change spectrum. What adjustments should you consider? Do you need to try harder? Try smarter? In a change process, sometimes we overshoot in order to reach a good target. We strive for an extreme so we don't slide back into our former situation. It's not a bad tactic as long as when we get to the Adjustment phase you acknowledge it. You are where you are. Maybe you want to move further toward the moon you set your sights on. That works, so go for it.

The categories of things you might need to adjust in the Adjustment phase are:

- Your expectations of:
    - Yourself
    - Others and the world
- Your reality:
    - Your thoughts
    - Your feelings
    - Your behaviors and tactics
- Your targeted change

Ready to tackle them one by one? I know you must be exhausted by the Action step, but without legitimate effort in the Adjustment step, all of your changes won't reach their full potential.

~ Your Expectations ~

You need to know what your expectations are before you determine where and how you might need to adjust. When we have expectations (of ourselves or others) that are removed from what reality is, we are setting ourselves up for disappointment. When we put our expectations on others it is a recipe for resentment. But, aren't expectations a part of life? We've let them be, but it's high time to kick them out.

In their place, create *agreements*. What's the big difference? *Expectations* are not based in reality, they are based in hope and assumptions. *Agreements* are grounded in cooperation and reality. You use your own volition and intentions in creating agreements. They contain your voice and you own them. You have to have communication to create them. You can choose to break them or keep them. Expectations run roughshod over choice and communication: They are usually "out there" without any form of discussion and certainly without agreement.

At this point in the change process, it's time to buckle down and get honest about whether or not expectations have reared their ugly head and driven you to go after something that really isn't yours to go after because it doesn't fit with what you agreed to do (or what is a reasonable fit with reality).

In this step, you get to modify your plan (if you didn't do so along the way). If you modified your plan along the way and are feeling somehow like you failed, get over it. Modifications are not (necessarily) sell outs. They are often necessary to move things forward, to take advantage of momentum and opportunity.

I once heard a sage piece of advice on adjusting expectations that stuck with me and I've been told again over and over: If you've got a solution for 80% of the problem, don't wait for the "right" (95%) solution that may arrive some distance down the road. If you tackle 80% of the problem and you're wrong about it, you can adjust your approach and still be solving the problem long before the 95% solution is established. Don't wait for perfect; pursue progress.

"Never discourage anyone who continually makes progress,
no matter how slow." ~ Plato

~ *Of Yourself* ~

When you embarked on this change process, were you realistic in your expectations of yourself? Were you born shy and your idea of a successful change process was to become the life of the party? Did you set your change agenda based on a perfect vision of yourself? Was your plan informed by other people who told you who and how you should be, but that's not a fit for you? Was the only way that you were going to implement a change was to work 24/7 and overcome objections of your entire department?

Now is the time to shift your expectations of yourself to create an environment for success. Here are some questions to challenge yourself with:

- Am I expecting myself to be perfect?
- Do I fail to recognize my own imperfections and am I not allowing some wiggle room for me to just "be?"
- Am I using other people's expectations of me (past or present) to define who I expect myself to be?

If you answered "yes" to one or more of those, you have some work to do. You need to actively let go of those harmful expectations if you want to be successful and happy. Contrary to popular thinking, being unreasonable and demanding in your expectations does not create beneficial results. Remember Acceptance? You need a dose of Acceptance of where you are and use the lessons you learned in Assessment to set reasonable expectations of yourself and others or this whole change chain is going to break, *fast.*

"Success consists of going from failure to failure without loss of enthusiasm." ~ Winston Churchill

~ Of Others & the World ~

Just recently, I was presenting on the topic of expectations to a women's group that I lead locally, and one of the women admitted that she throws expectations out like they are candy. Well, to be honest, that's not exactly what she said, but I read between the lines. What she *did* say was that she embraces feeling disappointed. She stated that she downright *enjoys* it.

Enjoys feeling *disappointed*? At first, I bristled at this, thinking that she was a bit crazy. Since I embrace some crazy in people, I let it wash over me and then it hit me: Expecting others to be who we <u>want them to be</u> instead of <u>who they are</u> leaves us with an ample dose of judgment about them. Judging others invites us to be elevated from others, which feeds our need for control, and our need for validation when others commiserate with us in our disappointment. When we feel that we are better than others, we feel better about ourselves and we are less likely to feel intimidated or insecure, at least on the outside. When we complain about others, we can share a common enemy with our inner circle (or colleagues) which makes us feel more secure and included.

So, how do our expectations of others fit into the change process and the Adjustment phase? If some of our change relies on others and what they do or don't do, and our expectations are some distance from reality (and any agreements we reached), we need to reconcile those differences right now. Are we expecting people to be different than they've proven themselves to be? Do we know someone who is chronically late? Are we getting mad every time they are late?

Please don't get me wrong: Being late is disrespectful. Getting angry when someone disrespects us is completely human. The problem arises when we act surprised when they do exactly what they always do. If one of our co-workers is habitually late for meetings, we can reasonably expect that they will be late for *our* meeting. If we delay starting the meeting, waiting for them to arrive, and get mad in the process, that's a waste of energy. We can choose to:

1. Keep getting angry.
2. Begin the meeting without them.
3. Wait for them but refuse to get angry about it.
4. Sit them down and create an agreement with them about their promptness.
5. Stop inviting them to meetings.
6. Bring it to the attention of our (or their) boss.

Reading that list might strike you as frustrating (until I got to the last one), given that I didn't give you any tools on how to fix their behavior. That's because you can't. You cannot hand this book to someone and make them change. You can invite, encourage, push, and cajole them to change. In the end, it's up to *them* as to whether or not to change. "You can lead a horse to water but you can't make him drink."

My life, both personal and professional, is littered with dehydrated horses. Expecting those horses to drink did nothing to make it so; all it did was make me anxious and irritable, resentful and distrusting. The person responsible for all of that nonsense? I'm looking at her in the mirror.

~ Coming To Terms With Loss ~

"The only way to get what you really want
is to let go of what you don't want." ~ Iyanla Vanzant

Facing up to the reality that you can't fix other people, no matter how hard you try, is hard. Similarly difficult is realizing that when you change and other people don't, they might reject you and your "new you." I've listened to a wide range of successful people who have the same story to share: When they started rising and expanding, their "friends" slipped (or ran) away. Some did so very dramatically ("how dare you?!") while others just disappeared.

You're going to suffer loss when you make changes. Some people won't like that you can or do change. It challenges them to be more than they are comfortable being. You might get accused of being self-centered or goody-two-shoes or something even more offensive. They might offer perceptions of you that are so far off base that you question your sanity momentarily.

Let them. You cannot change them or their minds. Their perceptions about you serve them. Their perceptions allow them to stay on the path they are on. To see you as YOU would be too costly for their safe zone. So let them go.

Now that we've covered expectations, it's time to discuss its awkward step-sister: Reality.

~ Your Reality ~

You can change *reality*? What?! Damn straight, you can. You can change the only reality that really matters: Yours.

When I was in graduate school, one of my absolute favorite professors, Robert Ryder, stirred a discussion on what "crazy" means. I was intrigued, especially given that several of my family members earned that clinical title. For me, crazy meant an aberration of reality or normalcy; not "fitting in." Changing your reality doesn't need to mean you're crazy. If you take deliberate steps to alter what you see it's often the sanest thing you can possibly do. Your reality changes with the decisions you make about what lens you'll place on the events and circumstances around you. You get to choose what you let in and what you push aside. Three people can watch the very same series of events and have very different interpretations of what happened. Those same three people can walk into a room and focus on entirely different cues and items. It's all in their filters.

I manage my filters closely. I don't watch the news. Any of it. How do I know what is going on in the world around me? Social media. My friends and colleagues let me know what I should pay attention to and investigate more. Even letting that toxic pipeline open as much as I do affects my energy and focus. If you ingest ick it makes you sick. Maybe the sickness comes through as anger or sadness or hopelessness. Maybe it doesn't affect you much because you are a pro at managing your filters. I

've gotten better over the years to not let a child kidnapping case in Oshkosh get up in my head so much that my entire day is trashed. I have to actively resist sliding down the rabbit hole of thinking that the entire world is an evil, awful place. When I think those things, my mood goes to Hell in a hand basket. My actions soon follow suit, with my motivation for creating more inspiration in the world dropping through the floor. When my filter is in check and I'm actively managing my own reality – what I choose to focus on – I'm in a better mental and emotional space and I make better, more powerful decisions. Take charge of your reality and see the immediate and long-lasting benefits.

~ *Of Your Thoughts* ~

"Your perception of life
really is your manifestation." ~ Abraham Hicks

How do you go about taking charge of your thoughts? As we discussed earlier in this book, you are the traffic cop of your brain.

You get to decide which thoughts stay and which thoughts get stopped dead in their tracks. Now that you're in the Adjustment phase, it's time to check in and see if your traffic cop has been on break? Are you consciously monitoring where your thoughts go, or are you allowing whatever nonsense flies into your head to take up residence? Are you playing victim to thoughts or are you planting them intentionally?

~ *Of Your Feelings* ~

In order to adjust your feelings, the first place to start is your thoughts. Let's suppose you're doing a bang-up job monitoring all of the thoughts that squeeze themselves into your noggin. As you now know, your feelings emerge directly from your thoughts, even when you aren't even conscious of them. Mopping up the mess of your overwhelming, self-defeating feelings comes directly after you lose track of the dysfunctional nature of your thoughts. If you start feeling crappy, the best thing to do is to rewind the clock and start rethinking things. Feelings aren't real. They are feelings and they may be warranted, but so may be another set of feelings altogether, depending on the assumptions we're making and the thoughts we are entertaining.

If you've gotten to this point in the change process and you're not where you wanted to be in terms of a transformation and you think your feelings are partly to blame, it's time to take stock. Are your feelings getting in the way of the change you envision? Are you feeling:

- Lethargic?
- Hopeless?
- Frustrated?
- Sad?
- Anxious?

If so, it's time to do some self-care exercises and return to the Action chapter to beef up on your skills on managing your feelings. Remember: Your feelings are not in control of you. You are in charge of your feelings.

~ *Of Your Behaviors & Tactics* ~

At the end of the thoughts-feelings-behaviors path is what you *do*. Assuming you've gotten to this point in the change process and you're not seeing the results that you hoped for, this step might be the key to adjust, assuming that your thoughts and feelings are supporting the change. Our past behaviors have created pathways (a.k.a. habits) that are tough to change. The biggest mistake we make is focusing on *changing* our behavior instead of focusing on the *new, desired* behavior. Did you do that? Were you so focused on resisting eating that bowl of ice cream that you "forgot" to focus on eating more healthy foods?

If you're a leader, ask your team "How can we change things to help you be more effective?" Return to the Action chapter to see what you might need to do more of. Are you sticking with your new habits? You can't do something once or twice and expect it to shift your behavior. You must create habits and new agreements with yourself and others about how you will behave and perform.

If you are not doing that in a positive way, circle back and re-commit to those changes. Admit your mistakes or missteps. Show your team that it is okay to slip and get back on course. When members can own up to their role in and contribution to the problem, there is great hope for individual and collective change. Buy into the change or no one else will. Without your commitment, it's just words on a page. Commit. This goes for your personal relationships, too. If you've committed to a change and you've slipped, don't exert energy covering it up. Face it, share it, and commit to do better.

~ Your Targeted Change ~

"The only failure is giving up." ~ Robin Sharma

Sometimes in life we find that the simplest answer is the correct one. Such might be the case with the question I'm about to pose to you: Did you try fixing the wrong thing?

Not too many years back, I had a coaching client who came to me with the story that she needed to help her son tackle a bunch of academic and life-management challenges. Her son was in his last year of college and had really messed some things up with a few of his classes, to the point where his graduation was questionable. She was feeling incredibly guilty because her son had just been through a rough patch personally and she felt that she didn't jump in soon enough or strong enough. She had been her "laid back" self and she vowed to be different. Her personal change agenda was built around her taking a front-seat role with her son.

The mom gave me detailed instructions on how to manage his affairs so he could be assured a successful outcome. These measures included talking with him and his advisor, checking his email (I was provided with the login and password), texting and emailing him daily, prepping him for each and every conversation he was to have with any University official, and being conferenced in during the conversations. See where this is going yet?

When I asked the mom what she wanted as an outcome, she listed: To get her son back on track, demonstrating better habits, and fixing all of his grades. Since this young man wasn't my son, it was easier for me to see how her coaching agenda was just a hair off target. This mom loved her son, of that I have zero doubt. She was also filled with fear that if every detail wasn't adequately managed, her son would fail and his life would be harshly affected in the short- and long-run. Her change agenda included two things that were very much on target:

Getting her son back on track and demonstrating better habits (organization, time management, etc.).

If she was reading this book at that juncture I'd have advised her to examine her change choice on one critical element of her change agenda: Fixing all of his grades. Why? Doesn't that sound reasonable? Won't good grades benefit her son? Of course it does, of course it will, but here's why it didn't belong on her change agenda: Because focusing her attention on trying to change his grades places her energy on something she can't control and would be better off not even trying to influence directly. She can mentor her son to advocate for himself *(influence)*, but she cannot *control* the changing of the grades. Her son can't assure that either. They both *can* focus on following the steps to get a grade change considered, and then focus on letting it go. Getting a "D" isn't great, but it's passing. It allows him to graduate.

It also offers a unique opportunity for her son to frame the reasons behind the bad grade(s); to speak to his imperfection and what he learned from not putting sufficient effort into his studies. If the grades get changed and are no longer a threat to his success, what has he learned?

When I discussed this with his mom she had a bit of a tough time swallowing that pill because she felt so responsible for "saving" her son. This behavior, however caring, wasn't doing her son any good. He needed to grow up and take charge of his own destiny, accepting responsibility for his stumbles. She needed to adjust her change agenda to replace "fixing his grades" to "accepting and working with his grades." She needed to craft her change agenda to focus on letting her son take responsibility for his own actions and moving into "witness" role.

Can you see yourself in this example? No, you don't have to have a struggling kid in college to see the mirror I've provided. Boiling it down, this example was all about correcting your change agenda by evaluating two things:

1. Are any of your change choices the responsibility of others (a mix-up of your control buckets), and you can only influence them?
2. Are any of the change choices under your control (acknowledging that others influence those things, too)?

If you are in control of your change choice (being more organized, taking better care of yourself physically, etc.), you're still called to examine how others may influence it (a spouse or co-worker messing up your clean workspace, tempting you with bad foods, or disrupting your gym routine). If your change choice is only under your *influence* (a company-wide change), you're called to focus only on your thoughts, feelings, and behaviors in response to the change. When you are aware of where to exercise your power, you can reserve it for where it means something and will make a true difference: First, over the things you can directly control (your thoughts, feelings, and behaviors), and second, over the things you can influence (the thoughts, feelings, and behaviors of others).

~ Bottom Line: Change Is Hard ~

Change is hard. It's possible, but it's hard. It's *really* hard sometimes. Your inner compass may tell you it just wants to go "home." It's time for me to share a story with you.

After the tearing down of the Berlin Wall and the fall of Communism in Eastern Europe in the late 1980s and early 1990s, I visited Russia as part of a volunteer trip organized by an intriguing organization called "EarthWatch™." Our group was staying in a southwest Russian village between Kazahtstan and the Ukraine documenting the religious practices of the babushkas (grandmothers). To get to this remote village, we had to travel by bus and train for the greater part of a day. Being from a comparatively urban area in the

U.S., I was intrigued by their culture and spent my time observing the interactions between the locals.

As we waited to board a bus, several people started getting into an argument, hollering things I couldn't understand, all in Russian, I assume. We finally boarded the bus and one of the women who had been part of the skirmish said something gruffly and plunked herself down in a seat. I pulled one of my counterparts aside and asked them to translate what she said. "It was better under Communism."

I'm not going to get into a political discussion because it's not my thing, but I will say that this was a powerful message. For this woman at least, the prospect of going back to the way things were was much more attractive than continuing to struggle through the adjustment to a new way of life.

You don't have to be plodding through the aftermath of a political transformation to feel the frustration that this woman felt after the change process started. It can be wholly uncomfortable. It's unfamiliar and uncharted territory. It creates new challenges that we may feel unsure how to best handle. We are out of our comfort zone and it can feel ugly. For some, it's exhilarating. It's a high to be riding the wave of change. I've found that these "change surfers" are a rare breed, and most of them wouldn't find a reason to read this book, so let's assume that's not you.

Saying that change is hard doesn't mean that it isn't worth it. Just that it's hard. Feel the frustration, just like you "felt the suck." There's no sense in denying it exists because it'll just push harder at your psyche to be paid attention to. It's okay to feel frustrated and even a bit disillusioned.

~ Deja Vu ~

"Nothing ever goes away until it has taught us
what we need to know." ~ Pema Chödrön

Stuck U.

Does it seem like you've been in this mess before? Is this not the first time you've tried to change and you keep ending up in the same spot? Are you having a case of déjà vu? It's time to break that pattern. If you've performed the steps in this book, you aren't seeing positive results, and you've been here before, it's time to establish what the common threads are so you can cut them.

How would you describe this "being in the same place?" What does that mean?

Did you do anything differently this time to get here? What did you do that was the same?

What does each path have in common? Did you rely on some of the same people? Did you spend a similar amount of time preparing for the change? Did you fall off track?

Remember that déjà vu isn't necessarily a bad thing. When we find ourselves in the "same" situations over and over again, yet we thought we had learned the lesson, we have to ask ourselves, "what happened?" We moved on our change journey: We went up a spiral staircase. As a result, we can look down on the experiences we had before, and the person we were then, and the mistakes and the triumphs. But we are different, and the lessons we can learn are slightly different. This is change. This is progress.

"No man ever steps into the same river twice,
for it's not the same river and he's not the same man." ~ Heraclitus

~ Learning From Our Mistakes ~

"The greatest glory in living lies not in never falling, but in rising every time we fall." ~ Nelson Mandela

In the time since my first book came out about needs, every time any friend brings up the topic of a need, they look over at me like I'm the needs expert. On my strong and clear days, I like to think that I'm the needs guru, the one that can pinpoint the solution to someone's pain. Then there are days that I'm almost immobilized by needs of my own that aren't being met. I'm going in cirlces. Fighting with myself over what I will give myself "permission" to need and what I will give up on. I'm angry and hurt.

In trying to remove myself from the emotional vortex I'd placed myself in, I reached out to a dear friend of mine. You know the friend – the one who tells you exactly what you don't want to hear but desperately need to. And she had this to say: "When are you going to stop putting your needs out there only to have them disregarded? When are you going to keep putting yourself in the position of wanting to be chosen, and not being chosen?"

If it's one thing I've learned over the years it's that old ghosts don't seem to die. For you literal types out there, I know, I know, ghosts can't *die*, that's what makes them *ghosts*. I've spent an immense amount of time in my life trying to slay them and have come to this conclusion: I *can* stop them from haunting me, but they never actually disappear. They are waiting in the hallways in the deep recesses of my mind, waiting for an opportunity to make their presence known if I am not resolute in changing patterns and practices that created the haunting in the first place.

We humans are so good at doing the same things over and over, hoping for different results. We find ourselves in situations, relationships, and circumstances that seem eerily familiar. Over and over and over again. We remain hopeful that THIS time it will be different. That THIS time we will not fall into that same trap that we've experienced repeatedly, to the point of exhaustion. Or madness. Then that fateful moment comes when that insightful friend you count on to cut through all the bull and give you the God's honest truth says, "Here you go again."

If you're anything like me, at first you're defensive, saying things like, "What? This is TOTALLY different than those other 100 bazillion times. I'm a COMPLETELY different person. I would NEVER do THAT again." But it's not so different. And you're not so different. And you have done it again.

I've been the spokesperson in my relationships for as long as I can remember. When my stepfather would rail against my mom, I would find myself stepping in, trying to take the heat. I'm pretty headstrong and have some fairly passionate opinions, so there's that, too. When I was in my late teens and early twenties I imagined making a living as a mediator, knowing how naturally I found myself in the middle. I have a deep-seated need for understanding and enlightenment in a professional advocate sort of way. Standing up for others makes me feel like I have a purpose. On first pass, this sounds all well and good, but there's more to the story.

Not too many years ago, I experienced a dismantling of my inner circle of "friends." (I used quotations because true friendships never would have taken the turns ours did.) Part of this drama involved two of the "weaker" people in our group. Please don't get me wrong: They had strength, but holding their voice and facing people's rejection of them were their soft spots. So, in steps Bridget, right into the belly of the beast. I was fighting other people's battles, trying to show community and strength through support.

Do you want to know how well that worked out? Not so well. In becoming the spokesperson, I became the target. I broke the rules of the group: Put lipstick on the pig and pretend nothing was wrong.

When I was cast out, I was quite hurt and angry that no one stood up for me the way that I stood up for them. After some thought about this, I realized it was no small wonder that they stayed quiet. Not only was it their comfort zone to stay quiet, I showed them how dangerous it can be to speak out against a system. I was a whistle blower. When you do that, you're a target. You're on the firing line. Most people prefer to stand by silently. They might dish behind people's backs, but face to face? That's rare.

What does this have to do with "Adjustment?" Over the years before this mess, I had been pursuing a path of enlightenment, inner strength, and calling people out on their dysfunction. I get paid to do it, for crying out loud! When this personal situation blew up I had to take responsibility for my part in it, or risk that it was all for nothing in the grand scheme of things. So, I did. I had forgotten a lesson from long ago: You can only help people who *want* to be helped. No one likes to be told that they are wrong when they have no interest in fixing it or changing. There I was shoving it in their faces like smelly garbage. No wonder they hated me! My adjustment? I made some new rules:

- Help only those who ask for help.
- Let others speak for themselves and experience their own path.
- Release my expectation that people will do for me as I do for them. They are them, I am me.

What new rules do you need to make? List them here and then start *doing* them. Rules I can make for myself that will give me more resolve, energy, and focus to change the things that I can control (list at least three):

1.

2.

3.

~ Tweaking For Success ~

If making large changes only requires small shifts, the Adjustment stage is much the same. You may need to just simply tweak what you did in the change process. Maybe you need to exert a little more effort or discipline? Maybe you need to slow down a little bit and focus more on your target? Or, maybe you have to really dig in because you have some underlying issues that aren't creating a climate for success? Ready to tackle those? Here are some sample questions to ask yourself:

What are you still tolerating that is getting in the way of your change efforts? How are your "tolerations" strengthening or weakening your resolve to stay in this better space/mentality? *Remember, tolerations are things that you are putting up with (bad habits, mental and physical clutter or distractions) that are weakening your focus and energy.*

Do you need to "clean house?" Are there relationships or employees or circumstances that need to be dumped in order for you to move forward effectively?

What help do you need to line up to assist you in making the changes you seek? A friend? A support group? A coach?

~ Finding A New Center ~

"Growth is painful. Change is painful.
But nothing as painful as staying stuck somewhere you don't belong."
~ Mandy Hale

Part of the Adjustment step is simply adjusting to a new you, or a new organization. You have to find comfort in a new homeostasis, a new center. Like going on a new health path, once you've lost the weight you need to keep the patterns that will keep it off.

A former client of mine came to me because she didn't have a "voice." Not literally, but figuratively. She had been letting other people run the show for her entire life. Slowly, and with a lot of guidance and encouragement, she started owning her own voice. She started telling people who tried to control her that she was not theirs to control. She was not property, she was her own person. She acted on that before she could articulate it. When she did articulate it, sometimes, especially at first, it came out emotionally and with lots of tears and yelling. Over time, as she owned it and reconciled what it meant for her (the changes and shifts and losses it had and would bring), she found more of her calm. She found her center.

What is your new center? What things do you need to keep doing repeatedly in order to maintain the changes you've made?

Feel free to list a few of those things here:

1.

2.

3.

Change is a continual process. There is no stopping. To quote one of my favorite movies of all time, *The Shawshank Redemption*, "Get busy living or get busy dying." If you're not growing, you're deteriorating. The truth of the matter is that we are born growing. As soon as we stop growing we start the track toward (literal) death. What we do in between is our choice. What are you going to do with that? Success doesn't come easy, but when you know what you're aiming for, you've got good equipment, taking the shot is much simpler.

~ Press On Or Opt Out ~

In this Adjustment step, you might just want to walk. You may want to throw in the towel and return to the status quo. As I used to say when I was going through a transformation of my own making years ago, "the only way out is through." I acknowledged, and experienced, that it often gets worse before it gets better. Like the Velveteen Rabbit™ analogy, becoming real is painful, but it's *real.* What if it's just too much to do? What's the trade off? Maybe you think you might be better off just staying exactly where you are because this change thing is a pain. Do you stand up to the challenge or walk away?

Well, don't just sit there: Let's figure it out!

What is the upside to staying the course and making this change? What is going to get better if I press on?

What is it going to cost me? Time? Effort? Friends? Some employee turnover? Risk?

So, what's it going to be, Champ? As your "paper" coach, I can't want the change more than you do. Or, to quote the philosophy of a personal trainer I once knew, "I can't care more about your fat ass than you do." How much do YOU care?

"When everything seems to be going against you, remember that the airplane takes off against the wind, not with it." ~ Henry Ford

~ Concluding Thoughts ~

What if you've gotten to this point in the book and you're not seeing the results you were seeking? Don't lose hope (in yourself or in my methods). I have some questions for you, to see if we can get to the heart of the matter. Is it possible that:

1. The tool isn't working 'cause you're not working the tool?

2. You didn't get buy-in from key stakeholders in the change process? Do the people affected by the change have a convincing answer to "what's in it for me?"

3. You stopped feeling invested in the change process after the Acceptance step? Maybe you didn't change because the source of the discomfort that got you to pick up this book was that you weren't accepting yourself as you are. Once you gave up the fight, the fight was gone.

Nothing comes out perfect the first time. Getting close to perfection takes practice and a whole lot of error and stumbling. Granted, you can minimize mistakes, but you cannot eradicate them. This chapter helped you to course-correct so that you can stay on track getting unstuck. Please don't be afraid to make corrections at this point in the process. I've seen a lot of people (and executives) let pride get the best of them and they skip this step entirely. They see that they need to adjust; instead, they gloss over the issues and pretend that they are set. Often, people get fired and companies reorganize after some time passes because it's assumed that the change effort failed. It didn't fail; it failed to get adjusted. Please don't be *that* guy or *that* company. Make the adjustments. Reap the bounty.

Key Chapter Concepts

- Three things you may need to adjust: Your expectations; your thoughts, feelings, behaviors; the targeted change itself.
- Come to terms with loss; decide if you want to press on or opt out.
- Learning from our mistakes is part of any good change process.
- Finding a new center…a new you…is a challenge and needs attention or you may slide back to the old ways. Systems and old habits are strong.

"Owning our story can be hard but not nearly as difficult as spending our lives running from it." ~ Brené Brown

PULLING IT ALL TOGETHER

"Opportunities don't open up to closed people." ~ Robin Sharma

Emotionally agile leaders – and individuals – will rule the world. It's not because they are power hungry or seek to oppress others; quite the contrary. Emotionally agile people desire and demand change because they recognize its potential to enlighten and transform the world. The world *can* change. Why do I believe this? Because I know that people can change, and the world is comprised of people.

This book has offered countless strategies and probing exercises designed to empower you to manifest change in whatever area of your life you desire. It's not going to be easy. It's going to require hard work and perseverance and guts. As a part of a greater organization, you're going to be challenged to work *smarter* not *harder* in order to keep agile as the economic landscape continues to shift and change. "Stuck U" gives you the tools to do just that. Use them. Please don't use just a handpicked few: Use all of them. Share them. Promote them. Make them a part of your corporate language and culture. Then, watch your organization move in ways you only dreamed possible.

To get the most out of your change process, you might need a accountability partner to help you. Coaches aren't miracle workers (okay, maybe *I am*, but *most* aren't). Coaches *are* accountability seekers and guides. We represent that "third eye" that helps us view ourselves from the outside when the noise and distractions confuse and overwhelm us. The best coaches *have* coaches, so we aren't immune from needing perspective either. If you've never worked with a coach, it's high time to invest in your growth and development. If you're an executive who has never hired an outside consultant, I cannot recommend it strongly enough. Systems are powerful entities and having an outsider to offer insights and challenge is critical to your success. I've provided you with a tome for change, and that may be enough for you to make it happen in your life, in your organization. If not, reach out. Build your accountability team and build your abundance.

What are you waiting for? Go open your Pipeline of Awesome and leave this beautiful, challenging, abundant, lacking, and fundamentally crazy world a better place for having given *you* life.

"You can waste your lives drawing lines.
Or you can live your life crossing them." ~ Shonda Rimes

ABOUT THE AUTHOR

"There is only one way to avoid criticism:
do nothing, say nothing, and be nothing." ~ Aristotle

Dr. Bridget Cooper is an experienced and dynamic organizational development consultant, retreat facilitator, and executive coach. Her drive is to help people to be clear, passionate, and invigorated about their lives and work so that they will propel their organizations toward success, establish stronger teams, healthy work climates, positive working relationships, and happier clients and customers. Her forte is developing and delivering custom-designed, interactive, and motivational, organizational development interventions taking the form of executive strategic planning retreats and conflict interventions as well as training seminars on: effective communication, conflict resolution, relationship building, productivity, finding your passion and purpose, time management, and decision making and problem solving. She has a proven track record of proactively, strategically, and effectively managing high-level organizational change and translating strategy into measurable objectives.

Through her education and experience, she understands relationship dynamics and approaches her work from a systemic and holistic perspective. She consults on leadership and entrepreneurial challenges for a variety of companies, and is practiced and available as a keynote speaker on any range of leadership and service topics.

She has conducted seminars and retreats and delivered keynotes for numerous associations and organizations including: Girl

Scouts of Connecticut, Vietnam Veterans of America, Women In Business Summit, Gateway Financial Partners, The Phoenix, Junior League of Washington, Department of Defense, Allied World Assurance Company, Believe, Inspire, Grow (B.I.G.) Connecticut, Connecticut Society of Association Executives, Glastonbury Chamber of Commerce, Connecticut Boards of Education, American Massage Therapists Association, CT Apartments Association, Metacon Gun Club, Women's Independence Network (WIN), Connecticut Associated Builders & Contractors, L-3 Communications, Hartford Dental Society, Bethany College, Draeger Medical Systems, The George Washington University, USA Weekend, TANGO, and American Case Management Association.

She has run a monthly empowerment workshop for women ("First Wednesdays") in addition to local presentations for Believe, Inspire, Grow (B.I.G.) of Connecticut for women entrepreneurs. She was selected as a special guest at "Game Changers Day 2015" at Lauralton Hall and was the featured closing keynote speaker for the 2015 Greater Hartford Women's Conference and guest speaker at the Women In Business Summit.

Raised in New England, she earned her B.S. with a concentration in human resource management from the University of Massachusetts, her M.A. in marriage and family therapy at the University of Connecticut, and her Ed.D. through the educational leadership program at the George Washington University. Her dissertation was on the social network structures of women in academic medicine.

Dr. Cooper been a leader in the Girl Scout organization, President of the Parent-Teacher Organization, soccer coach, religious education instructor, and elementary school room parent and activity chairperson. Prior to her move to Connecticut, she served as an instructor in conflict resolution and anger management for inmates of the Fairfax County Adult Detention Center. Her hobbies include fumbling around on the guitar, traveling to places far and wide, and seeking out photo opportunities of people, places, and things. She has a never-ending bucket list that she's slowly checking off, and she takes suggestions.

She has two other books aimed at assisting organizations and individuals solve their personal and interpersonal challenges. Her book, *Feed The Need* (2013, 2014), will change the way you think about problems, and strengthen and empower you to solve them. In this groundbreaking book, you will discover how to identify, understand, and feed your core emotional needs so that you can live more harmoniously with yourself and others and resolve any conflict more effectively. She adapted this guide for teenagers in *Feed The Need: Teen Edition* (2014), with a foreword written by a high school student. Please contact her to gain her insight and partnership on solving your personal, professional and organizational challenges at bridget@piecesinplace.com.

Testimonials about Dr. Cooper's Consulting, Seminars, & Keynotes:

"I've been attending and running leadership retreats for many years and Bridget is by far the most effective facilitator I've ever experienced." *Board Member, Connecticut Society of Association Executives*

"I will be recommending you to everyone I speak to. This was the best Board retreat I've ever been to, and I've been to a lot over the years." *Board Member, Glastonbury Chamber of Commerce*

"You changed, and saved, my life." *Coaching Client, Florida*

"With Bridget on my team, I now have a Coach that leads me to be a leader. I had ideas when we began, I now create ideas. I had goals when we began, I now achieve. I had thoughts when we began, I now dream. And what's most awesome: I am led to live my dream." ~ *Executive Coaching Client, Colorado*

"Bridget is one of those people that carries a sense of calm with her no matter the audience she faces. As a person, she is intuitive, a phenomenal listener, and a positive spirit. As a consultant, she is a critical thinker that captures the essence of what is happening in real time in order to translate it in a meaningful way for all participants." *Associate Director, TANGO*

"I have had the great fortune to work with Bridget on a few different occasions and am better off as a result. Bridget has a unique and distinct knack for very quickly becoming a member of the team(s) she is working with, giving her a great deal of trust and camaraderie with the group. Bridget, without fail, stays focused on result, even if it means changing course during our sessions. Her goal isn't just to follow a script, sadly an experience I have had in some cases, but rather to involve herself in the team and work to result. I'm confident when I learn that Bridget is facilitating any meetings that they will be quite successful! Bridget's personality, in my opinion, is another factor that will continue to set her apart. As mentioned earlier, she gets acquainted with those she is working with, allowing her to blend at a somewhat personal level while maintaining very high standards of professionalism and integrity." *VP of Information Technology, Draeger Medical Systems*

"You know our audience well and your exceptional ability to engage our leaders in apt discussions on a range of topics critical to their performance…has proven to be invaluable." *President, Vietnam Veterans of America*

"Bridget's listening, prompting, pushing, and cajoling in a way that brought out the best in every attendee, resulted in action plans that insure that our organization tackles the important issues." *Executive Director, Connecticut Society of Association Executives*

"Ten hours with Bridget is better than 100 hours with my therapist!" *Client, Virginia*

"I wish to express my gratitude for all of the work and expertise you put into the presentation at our conference. I will enjoy reading your book and thanks for autographing it to me. Your brought your A-game (I don't see you being able to bring anything else) and your energy to make our conference informative, entertaining and delightful to be at." *Seminar Participant, Chicago, IL*

"I had the pleasure of working with Bridget twice. After experiencing her facilitation of our complicated, executive management meeting I contacted her soon thereafter to run my team's "off-site". In Bridget's role as facilitator of the Executive Management meeting, she did a masterful job of getting the participants to agree on overall objectives and 'rules'. This served us well for the two days of discussions and set the framework for Bridget to keep the team away from the volatile, emotional side topics that would have derailed us and focused us on resolving the challenging problems in front of us. As the facilitator of my team's offsite, Bridget was a quick study in assessing each team member's strengths, weaknesses, and aspirations. In addition, she worked closely with me to set the meeting format and objectives, with the right amount of direction and guidance without forcing her perspective. Throughout the meeting, Bridget effectively led the team through the discussions and to a worthwhile conclusion, managing a wide array of personalities and handling each one in a way so that their input was obtained and overall buy in was achieved. Bridget is very insightful, approachable, and very helpful at bringing teams through difficult discussions to actionable conclusions." *VP of Product Management, Draeger Medical Systems*

"I really enjoyed and was inspired by your spirit and passion for getting those messages of hope to us. You filled our cup!" *Attendee, First Wednesdays.*

My Last Page

Pete, The Smiley Face (younger bro, Steve ☺)

From my daughter…opening up her inner awesome. ♡